The ART of CARICATURE

The Author

The ART of CARICATURE

DICK GAUTIER

A PERIGEE BOOK

Perigee Books
are published by
The Putnam Publishing Group
200 Madison Avenue
New York, NY 10016

The author gratefully acknowledges permission from the following
sources to reprint material in their control:

Phaidon Press Ltd., Oxford, England, for material from *The Mirror
of Art* by Charles Baudelaire, translated by Jonathan Mayne,
copyright © 1955 by Phaidon Press Ltd., Oxford.

Charles Scribner's Sons for drawing of William Howart Taft
and poem from *Confessions of a Caricaturist* by Oliver Herford,
copyright 1917 Charles Scribner's Sons, copyright renewed 1945.

Library of Congress Cataloging in Publication Data

Gautier, Dick.
The art of caricature.

"A Perigee book."
Bibliography: p.
Includes index.
1. Caricature—History. 2. Cartooning—
Technique. I. Title.
NC1325.G39   1985   741.5   85-9462
ISBN 0-399-51132-6

Printed in the United States of America
3   4   5   6   7   8   9   10

Acknowledgments

I really had no intention in the world of writing a book until my good friend and fellow actor-artist Dave Madden (of *The Partridge Family, Laugh-In,* and *Alice* fame) came to me with the suggestion. For that and for many hours of help and encouragement I warmly thank him.

I'm also grateful to (shades of George Orwell) a couple of machines. If I didn't have my trusty Epson QX-10 to help me organize my research and process my words and a Victor 6040 printer to print them out for me, I would still be in my office, wading waist deep in papers, searching for a stub of pencil.

I must also thank my wife Barbara. (Can you imagine the havoc around the house if I didn't?) During the writing and illustrating of this book, she was patient and tender—and the owner of a genuine cattle prod. Her ploy of swapping coffee and a Twinkie for each completed page was nothing short of brilliant.

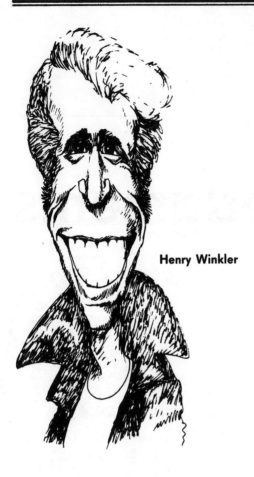

Henry Winkler

Luciano Pavarotti

Contents

Foreword

When Dick Gautier asked if I would be interested in writing the foreword to his book, I immediately accepted—without even knowing what the book was about. After all, Dick is an old friend and colleague, one of the most gifted actor-comedians in the country, and I find it difficult to refuse anything he asks. (Well, not exactly "*any*thing." Okay, Edgar?) My first thought was that the book would be about the nature of comedy or something like that and that Dick, being an old friend and colleague, would naturally have some flattering things to say about *his* old friend and colleague. Well, it turned out I was half wrong. I read the book—as I assume you are about to do—and although I searched like a crazy lady, I couldn't find anything flattering about me. Especially that caricature of me on the next page. Well, so much for old friendships and old colleagueships.

But when I said above that I was *half* wrong, I meant that: No matter what this book is called, it *is* about comedy. A different and perhaps higher form of comedy than what we might see at the Improv or on the Johnny Carson Show, but what a caricaturist does is essentially the same thing I and many other professional comedians do. We poke fun. Sometimes gently, sometimes not so gently. People who achieve fame and wealth through public approval must also accept the risk of public criticism and just plain public iconoclasm. The caricaturist and the comic are really blood brothers and/or sisters. We both tend to see reality as if reflected in a fun-house mirror, and our achievement is measured by how skillfully and entertainingly we can communicate that vision to an audience. The trouble comes

Joan Rivers

in trying to explain that particular creative process, that business of translating a mental perception into a visual image or verbal impression. I really believe that Dick has overcome that problem beautifully in this book. Not only does he tell us—in highly readable fashion—about the history of the caricature, he puts us into the heads of the caricaturists themselves and allows us to share in their unique visions. Beyond that, he provides us a generous sampling of the art itself and painstakingly teaches us how to put pencil to paper fearlessly and creatively. Other than some explicit sex scenes, what more could you ask for?

The only personally depressing aspect of the book is that it left me totally depressed. I mean, there's very little possibility that in two hundred years anybody will have one of my monologues hanging on the wall. Or even included in a book as good as this one. It's obviously Edgar's fault. The first time I said "Can we talk?" any husband with a shred of compassion would have said, "Joanie, make it— 'Can we draw?'"

JOAN RIVERS
September 1984

Don Rickles

Prince

Liza Minnelli

Robert Mitchum

Robert Vaughn

Rodney Dangerfield

Rudolf Nureyev

Stevie Wonder

Edward Kennedy

Sam Wanamaker

Willie Nelson

Cantinflas

Princess Diana and Prince Charles

Telly Savalas

Sissy Spacek

Lionel Richie

The ART of
CARICATURE

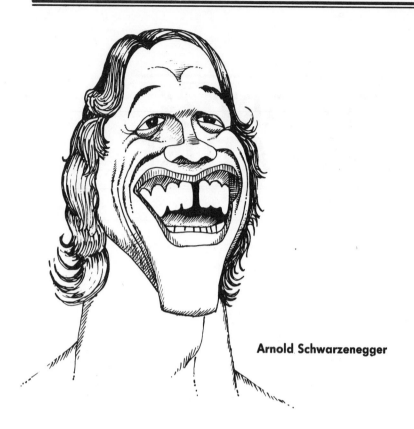

Arnold Schwarzenegger

Burt Reynolds

Introduction

While Art was threading its way through history, carefully producing serene still lifes, idyllic landscapes and stiff portraits, its poor bastard cousin caricature was waging war on corruption, injustice and hypocrisy. Caricature has always taken on the bullies; it's the nature of the art. It makes us laugh and it makes us think. Anything that can accomplish that is okay in my book.

I've been hooked on caricature for as long as I can remember. I'm a sucker for a good funny drawing, and proud of it.

Caricature is the art of tweaking noses, of needling. It's the great equalizer; no face can withstand its scrutiny without crumbling before its power—humor. And yet it seems to me the quintessential form of protest, the most civilized method of unleashing and rechanneling hostility.

Caricature is deceptively simple on the surface, but its strength lies in that apparent simplicity. Caricature cuts through boundaries of social station, literacy and intellect and ultimately finds its target. Its prodding art can supersede the written word. When "Boss" Tweed was wriggling under the penetrating pen of Thomas Nast, he was heard to say, "I didn't care a straw for your newspaper articles, my constituents don't know how to read, but they can't help seeing those damn pictures."

That's what this book is about—those damn pictures. We'll trace their origins in antiquity and follow them up to the present day. This will not be a dusty, dull chronology. I've tried to fashion a book that I myself would like to read, and since I have a rather limited attention span, I've tried to keep it engrossing, enlightening and entertaining. Think of it as a casual stroll through caricature's garden, stopping now and then to admire one flower and inhale the fragrance of another. Along the way we'll hear from some of the world's foremost caricaturists; these Peck's bad boys of the art world will offer us fresh insights into the slightly warped minds of those valiant souls who get up every morning and draw funny pictures for a living.

Later on, I'm really going to stick my neck out as I lay out a series of steps, shortcuts and suggestions—a formula, if you will—to aid and encourage the aspiring caricaturist and/or frustrated amateur.

But, you might rightfully ask, what is an actor doing writing a book about caricature? Well, I'm an inveterate, compulsive doodler, and, I might add, thank God for it. During some of the lean times in show business (acting is not always what it's cracked up to be) I was able to ferret out a badly needed buck or two as an illustrator, cartoonist and designer—and yes, of course, a caricaturist. But then, "any art in a storm."

So this book is the culmination of a lifelong love affair with this belligerent, often misunderstood art. Yes, I do call it art and already I can hear murmurs of protest from some quarters. I merely want to share with you, the reader, my unbridled enthusiasm for caricature and maybe even goad you into taking a crack at it yourself.

Caricature is admittedly easy to dismiss—it is a thing of the moment. Exaggeration is caricature's stock-in-trade, and since exaggeration is a simple form of humor, there is a tendency to denigrate it. But then all art is exaggeration: intensification of light or color or shape. Caricature is merely a more specific application of that technique with humor thrown in for good measure.

Annibale Carracci wrote in the sixteenth century:

> Is not the caricaturist's task exactly the same as that of the classical artist? Both see the lasting truth beneath the surface of mere outward appearance. Both try to help nature accomplish its plan. The one may strive to visualize the perfect form and to realize it in his work, the other to grasp the perfect deformity, and thus reveal the very essence of a personality. A good caricature, like every work of art, is more true to life than reality itself.

And it has always been thus. Ever since caricature emerged from the playful psyche of primitive man, it has been provocative, piquant, fascinating and fun. I sincerely hope this book lives up to its subject matter.

The Beginnings

What is caricature, exactly? I don't think anyone knows—exactly. I thought I knew when I embarked upon this adventure, armed only with my curiosity, my library card and a spiral notebook. But the more I read about caricature, the more dissension raised its ugly, niggling head.

Caricature has, at one time or another, been accused of being everything: trivial, trenchant, pithy, purposeless, charming, childish—interestingly enough, everything but dull. Caricature has always managed to kick up clouds of controversy. It has confounded the critics, punctured the pompous and, more often than not, ruffled the feathers of the famous and infamous.

It has been labeled non-art, sub-art, demi-art, pop art; and yet, while other artistic fads flare up and fade away, caricature doggedly clings to the public's affections.

And the definitions are as diverse and as profuse as the approaches to the art itself. For example:

> A caricature is a ludicrous exaggeration or distortion of characteristic or peculiar features. (Webster's Dictionary)

> Caricatures are often the truest history of the times. (Ralph Waldo Emerson in his *Journal*)

Caricature is the philosophical analysis of the comic element . . . an esthetic speaking tube or trumpet. (Eduard Fuchs in *The World in Caricature)*

. . . putting the face of a joke upon the body of a truth. (Joseph Conrad)

The most perfect caricature is that which, on a small surface with the simplest means, most accurately exaggerates, to the highest point, the peculiarities of a human being at his most characteristic moment. (Max Beerbohm in "The Spirit of Caricature")

Parodies and caricatures are the most penetrating of criticisms. (Aldous Huxley)

Destruction of beauty and regularity by exaggerated characterization; that is caricature (Hermann Müller)

Caricature is always us against them. The joke is shared; so is the hate. (William Feaver in *Masters of Caricature)*

See what I mean about disagreement? But then, caricature is a notorious catalyst for controversy. It has straddled a razor-thin line between "high" art and popular cartoon for centuries and only recently has it found a comfortable, though perhaps less powerful, niche for itself.

This is possibly why many critics have not been kind to caricature. It's too elusive; they can't pin it down and consequently they feel uncomfortable dealing with it. Because it is an art of the moment, they choose to brand it as trivial, "as fleeting as yesterday's headlines." It's true that all caricature, though reflecting the passions of the times, does not always achieve eternal significance.

Charles Baudelaire, in his essay "L'Essence du Rire," observed:

In caricature, even more than in the other arts, there exist two kinds of work, precious and commendable for different—almost contradictory reasons. Some have value merely because of the fact that they represent something: these, no doubt, merit the attention of the historian, the antiquarian, even the philosopher; they should take their place in the national archives and in the biographic records of human thought. As with the ephemeral of journalism, they are carried away by the very winds that brought them and, in their place, bring fresh novelties. But the others—the others bear within themselves an element mysterious, eternal, and this commands the attention of the artist.

So the critics continued to praise innocuous, albeit well-crafted, paintings of bowls of fruit while turning their backs on caricature, that "trivial," illegitimate form of art. And yet that trivial art was helping to elect Presidents; it was swaying public opinion with devastating results; it was exposing scandal in high places and

Head of Christ (end of eleventh century).

Hawaiian god of war.

even caused several anti-cartoon bills to be presented before various state legislatures. Just for the moment, let's assume that the critics are right, and that caricature is frivolous, an empty, easy joke. Don't we require a measure of that in our lives? Don't we have to leaven the weightiness of everyday living with a healthy dose of trivia?

Harvey Mindess, in his book *Laughter and Liberation*, agrees: "Nonsense—a trivial, frivolous form of wit brings freedom and renewed vitality to the most mature developed minds." And so it is with caricature; it's reassuring for us to see a powerful politician, for instance, cut down to size by caricature. It brings him down from his carefully manufactured partisan pedestal so we can deal with him in less deified terms: Yes, he does have pimples and flaws. The continuing success of caricature in America is a constant testament to our healthy capacity for self-criticism.

Humor in art has always fought an uphill battle. The comedic artist, performer and writer have consistently gotten the short end of the stick (or shtik, if you will). Perhaps the nature of the art demands that it be accomplished with apparent ease and this, in turn, makes its critics believe that comedy is in fact easy. Nothing could be further from the truth. It takes the skilled caricaturist years to sharpen his eye, and train his hand, in order to produce a fine sketch in a relatively short time. But then we often make the mistake of equating good work with long, hard work.

Nick Meglin writes in *The Art of Humorous Illustration*:

> Somewhere along the line, humor in art has been dealt a deadly blow. Those who determine taste (perhaps the most enigmatic word in our language) have decided it's all right for an artist to move us to tears, revolt and, in some cases, sleep—but to laugh is beneath an artist's station. Satirical work like that of Daumier can be excused: satire is an acceptable vehicle for prompting serious thought. Humor for humor's sake, however, is considered low brow, hence, the lack of it on museum walls.

And caricature does not hold the exalted place it once enjoyed. At one point in

Hellenistic masks of comedy and tragedy.

28

Paleolithic sculpture.

history, and I know this is hard to believe, it caused near riots in the streets. Just read what this Frenchman wrote in London in 1802:

> If men be fighting over there [in France] for their possessions and their biases against the Corsican robber, they are fighting here to be the first in Ackermann's shop and see Gillray's latest caricatures. The enthusiasm is indescribable when the next drawing appears; it is a veritable madness. You have to make your way in through the crowd with your fists. . . .

Sounds more like a rock concert than a flock of Englishmen eager for a peek at a new drawing, but that was the effect and power that caricature once possessed.

Today caricature continues to dish it out in a quieter but still effective way in the hands of such talented artists as Al Hirschfeld, David Levine, Edward Sorel and others. Perhaps it does not evoke the passionate enthusiasm it once did, but then how could it? The mass media have taken their toll. During caricature's heyday, the eighteenth and nineteenth centuries, the average citizen was not inundated with the same multiplicity of images as we are today, and consequently each image was held more dear and thus retained its potency. In this highly accelerated, technologically advanced world, we are exposed to television, billboards, motion pictures, magazines, newspapers—even the skies offer us messages: all importuning us, selling us, telling us, warning us, tempting us, luring us. We are probably exposed to more man-made images in one day than our eighteenth-century counterparts encountered in a lifetime. So caricature has lost most of its impact by sheer dint of numbers.

But caricature must be, as the psychologists say, a basic mimetic instinct. It has reared its head, in one form or another, with no societal prompting, in nearly every country, clan, sect and tribe in the world. Whenever the individual began to gain stature, caricature conveniently appeared on the scene to keep him honest, to cut him back to size. It's a wonderfully cathartic way to deal with the repressions of structure and authority, to strike out at hypocrisy and pretense. After all, isn't that exactly what we did when we immortalized our English Lit teacher with a Ticonderoga No. 2 in the margins of our notebooks?

Sigmund Freud equated caricature with unmasking, as though the drawing were a peeling away of external artifices to reveal the real person underneath. He

A Roman soldier used red chalk to do this simple drawing on the walls of his barracks in Pompeii. It happened to be the twenty-third of August, the year was A.D. 79, and Mount Vesuvius conveniently erupted, thereby preserving for us one of the world's first caricatures.

This portrait in stone of Ikhnaton, King Tutankhamen's unpopular father-in-law, dates back to about 1360 B.C., and is generally accepted as the earliest remaining caricature. Isabel Simeral Johnson writes in her book *Caricature and Cartoon* that "Ikhnaton's features were so abnormally ugly that it is difficult to tell a caricature of him from an authentic portrait." Egyptologists have recently theorized that Ikhnaton was a victim of acromegaly or some other feature-distending disease. So the first caricature may not be a caricature after all.

felt caricature accomplished more than merely aggressively making fun of someone: It revealed one's true nature. Freud also stated that "caricature is directed at objects who command authority and are popularly believed (on a lesser or greater scale) to be exalted in some sense." And this is a major part of caricature's appeal. Its prime targets are those who have achieved high position and have swelled to blimplike proportions through an exaggerated sense of their own importance. The bigger the blimp, the louder the pop when the caricaturist's pen punctures it.

Caricature, this intrinsic part of man's nature, is as old as man himself. Although primitive man didn't know it, the moment he imitated his neighbor's bowlegged stance, his voice or even the way he dragged his mate into the cave, he was indulging in a form of caricature. When our ancestors developed manual dexterity and learned the art of wielding a charred stick, the graphic arts were born—and caricature wasn't far behind. Caricatures have been found on the walls of caves where some early artist scratched an unflattering likeness in stone in order to mock his quarrelsome neighbor. Ernst Kris and E. H. Gombrich write in their essay "The Spirit of Caricature," that the latent goal of fun, including caricature, is concerned with magic. To mimic a person, to copy and ridicule his traits, is to destroy his individuality, much like the Indian belief that a photograph removes a portion of the soul.

Caricature, in various forms, appears in ancient and medieval art and writings. The Greeks and Romans were fond of picturing their gods in ridiculous poses, as

In 1233, some anti-Semitic clerk in a public record office in London drew this caricature attacking Isaac of Norwich, a rich Jewish merchant who had lent great sums of money to abbots, bishops and vicars.

In 1490, Leonardo da Vinci drew these five grotesque heads that appear to be pure caricature. Some scholars disagree: Giorgio Vasari, the sixteenth-century artist and biographer, claimed that Leonardo drew a faithful representation of a group of deformed men.

Much of the credit (or blame) for the spread of caricature as a formulated art must go to Annibale Carracci who, with his brother Agostino and cousin Lodovico, opened a school of painting in Bologna in the sixteenth century. Carracci (the similarity to "caricature" is mere coincidence) taught a conservative version of the Baroque style, stressing low-key lighting and deep shadows. He encouraged his students to study the masters of the Renaissance: Michelangelo, Raphael and others. However, in between their lessons, the students began to indulge in a form of diversion designed to lessen the tensions of "high" art. This visual play involved depicting the frequent visitors to the studio as various animals, or as inanimate objects. These people were amused and flattered to see their likenesses on the bodies of pigs, asses, dogs, jugs and even loaves of bread.

Martin Luther was the first to recognize and use the power of caricature for political purposes. He had some skill as an artist himself, and along with his good friend the painter Lucas Cranach, Luther published a pamphlet of woodcuts by Cranach attacking and ridiculing the pope in the name of Protestantism. Referring to the Cranach drawings, Luther wrote, "Maddened the pope with those pictures of mine, have I. If anyone feels hurt, I'm ready to justify them before the whole empire. Ah, how the sow will stir the dung. And when they've done for me, they'll go on dung eating just the same."

No drawing was too gross for Luther's taste as long as it conveyed his passionate message. In response, the opposition enlisted artists like Erhard Schön, who pictured Martin Luther as an instrument being played by the devil. This is reputedly the first widely circulated caricature of a specific recognizable person.

were the Hindus. The Orientals had a penchant for attaching animal characteristics to their human figures. The Romans felt that to affix long tails or animal heads to respected members of the community would reduce them to absurdities. Even carved African masks were actually caricatures designed to ward off evil spirits, perhaps by laughing at them. Aristotle mentions an artist named Pauson who suffered greatly for the drawings he did of the social elite. Caricature was a social talent then, like playing the piano today. It was permissible to ridicule the common man, but the social hierarchy would not brook being made to look absurd. Pliny the Elder tells us about Bupalus and Athenis, a pair of sculptors who taunted Hipponax, an extremely ugly poet, by publicly exhibiting a derogatory portrait of him. In retaliation, the homely poet wrote a verse about the sculptors so devastatingly cruel that it ultimately led them to hang themselves in double despair. But then, not everyone accepts criticism gracefully.

So you see, caricature is hardly a newcomer to society; the form has been around much longer than the word itself. The word *caricature* did not even find its way into an English dictionary until 1755. The English borrowed it from the French, who had added it to their vocabulary in the early part of the eighteenth century by way of the Italian *caricatura*, which means the art of exaggeration. *Caricatura* came from *caricare*, meaning to overburden or load, as in a loaded statement. A *caricatura* was also called a *ritratto carico*, or "loaded" portrait.

Caricature recalls the word *character* (from the old French *caractère*). We

Pier Leone Ghezzi became the toast of Rome with his caricature portraits. He was known as the *"famoso cavaliere delle caricature."* The social elite felt slighted if not victimized by Ghezzi's pen. At this time caricature was still a personal art, a social talent like playing the piano.

should also keep in mind here the Italian *cartone*, which is pasteboard, the heavy paper upon which artists drew. *Cartone* later veered off in another direction and ultimately became *cartoon*, which even today refers to the simple preliminary sketch that artists did for a fresco or mural. To recapitulate: The English took from the French who borrowed from the Italians. This is one creation the Russians have not laid claim to—as yet.

Oddly enough, all political, satirical, humorous or grotesque drawings were called caricatures until about 1843. Mr. Punch, in response to an exhibit of artists' designs intended for the new House of Parliament, facetiously called his political caricatures "cartoons": the word has been applied ever since. Time has now narrowed the meaning of caricature for us. Today it denotes "any exaggerated, often humorous, likeness of a specific individual."

The English

Though William Hogarth is generally acknowledged as the father of modern caricature, it is a title he would have scorned. The French novelist and art collector Champfleury called him the "first king" and the "true father of caricature," but Hogarth in his *Analysis of Beauty* denied vehemently that he was a "caracturer." He viewed with undisguised contempt the Italian *caricatura,* considering it shallow and unfaithful to his own high standards of art. Hogarth once wrote that "shows of all sorts gave me uncommon pleasure when an infant . . . and mimicry, common in all children, was remarkable in me." This peculiar talent for imitation was indeed remarkable, for although he did not use specific personalities in his drawings, nor always avail himself of particular events, he did have the perspicacity to view mankind's foibles and follies, and to place them in a timeless capsule for future generations to enjoy. Unlike many caricaturists whose works were only of the age, Hogarth produced works destined to live forever.

Hogarth was, in fact, a history and portrait painter who attempted to escalate humor in art. He felt it did not deserve its low status and tried to reform the views of its staunchest critics. By today's standards Hogarth could be labeled extremely right-wing, as he was opposed to any kind of social reform. His only foray into the political arena, in 1762, so angered his former friends the politician John Wilkes and the poet Charles Churchill that Hogarth was unmercifully harassed by them until the end of his days.

One of Hogarth's subjects, a rather homely yet paradoxically vain man, was so

William Hogarth's "Characters & Caricaturas."

outraged at the lifelike portrait that Hogarth did of him that he refused to pay the artist. Hogarth quickly responded with this note: "If you do not call and pay for the portrait I have made of you forthwith, I shall add a tail to it, along with other simian appendages and have the portrait exhibited at your club." I think the phrase "other simian appendages" did the trick. Hogarth was promptly paid.

Hogarth wrote:

> *Caricatura* is, or ought to be, totally divested of every stroke that hath a tendency to good Drawing. . . . Let it be observed, the more remote in their Nature the greater is the Excellence of the Pieces; as a proof of this, I remember a famous *Caricatura* of a certain Italian singer, that Struck at first sight, which consisted only of a Straight perpendicular Stroke with a Dot over it.

Hogarth paved the way for James Gillray, Thomas Rowlandson, the Cruikshanks and others. The sudden emergence of caricaturists on the scene was a direct result of the Bloodless Revolution of 1688–89; the power of the monarch had been lessened considerably, and artists took full advantage of the new freedom afforded them. Gillray used his acerbically witty drawings to expose the evils of the Hanoverian regime. He is regarded as the first artist to utilize the medium fully as a castigatory, political tool.

James Gillray's "Armed Heroes."

NASHIONAL TASTE !!!
(dedicated, without permission, to the Church Commissioners —

Isaac Cruikshank's "Nashional Taste!!!"

It was due to Gillray's superb craftsmanship and keen insight that England came to be known as the House of Caricature. Napoleon became the most caricatured person of his time; this was due in no small part to Gillray. His pen fashioned a comical portrait of an angry dwarf festooned with military accoutrements, ranting and raving his way across Europe; it was to become a quintessential simulacrum of that era. It was Gillray's drawings that drove the crowds mad outside Ackermann's shop; the artist was the darling of his time, as well as a major influence on the caricature of today. About Gillray's persistent attacks on "Little Boney," Champfleury wrote: "Bonaparte had for adversary the pitiless Gillray, veritable incarnation of John Bull, who roused the fibres of patriotism."

The Cruikshanks—Isaac, the father, and George and Robert, the sons—were the only working trio that caricature has ever produced. Isaac took Gillray's lead and continued to pummel Napoleon with a series of devastating drawings. He helped to formulate the Corsican into the figure we now know: the sulky stance, the one hand lost inside the oversized coat, the wide hat perched atop a dark swatch of bangs.

Isaac was unfortunately a pen for hire and would ruthlessly oppose any faction with his artistic abilities if the price was right. At one time he was offered one hundred pounds to back away from his anti-royalist campaign. He took the money

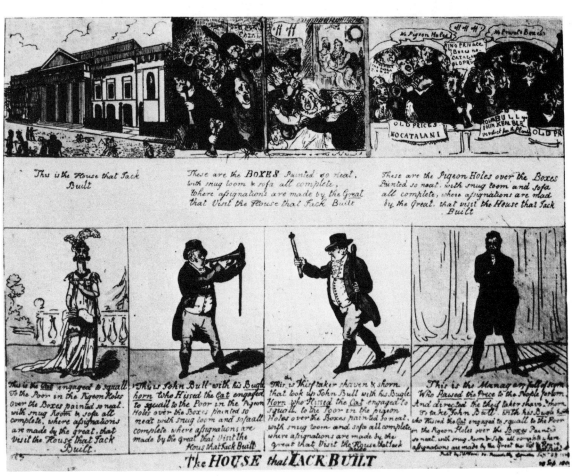

"The House that Jack Built" by Isaac Cruikshank and his son George.

The LADIES ACCELERATOR

Robert Cruikshank's "The Ladies Accelerator."

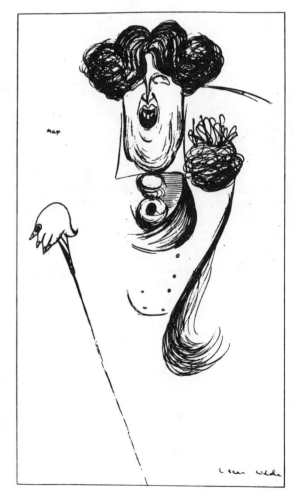

Max Beerbohm (Sir Max after 1939) was a gentle, whimsical caricaturist who captured the fancy of the readers of *Vanity Fair* magazine. His breathy, gentlemanly style reflected the genteel emotional climate of England at the time. Beerbohm did not take his drawing ability very seriously; he wrote, "Caricaturing is pure instinct without any trouble at all." Here is his drawing of Oscar Wilde.

For all of his wit, Oscar Wilde did not take kindly to caricature. Toulouse-Lautrec, who began his career as a cartoonist, James Whistler, Ape (Carlo Pellegrini) of *Vanity Fair* and the great Max Beerbohm all pictured Wilde as an overweight, effeminate snob. This caused Wilde to remark, "Caricature is the tribute that mediocrity pays to genius."

In fact, when Wilde saw Whistler's sketch, he groaned, "It's a pretty poor work of art." Whistler countered with, "And you're a pretty poor work of nature."

Whistler, known primarily for his famous painting of his mother (actually entitled *Arrangement in Grey and Black No. 1.*) was a mercurial Bohemian who fought with everyone. He once sued John Ruskin after the critic described his nocturne painting of the Thames as "flinging a pot of paint in the public's face." After a heated, well-publicized trial, Whistler won and was awarded . . . one farthing. Here is Whistler's "Oscar Wilde." Scholars have recently opined that it may have been drawn by Whistler's wife Beatrice. Nevertheless it is a Whistler. Reprinted by permission of The Hunterian Art Gallery, University of Glasgow, Birnie Philip Bequest.

and then continued, in an oblique way, to suggest the guilt of the royalists just the same.

George, the next Cruikshank, became an outstanding caricaturist of his generation and, unlike his father, he did not suffer from venality. He was initially anti-government, but he soon grew to adopt a very conservative posture. He eventually turned to the risk-free, apolitical world of illustrating books designed for the family trade. His brother Robert, though not as famous today, was nonetheless a prolific and successful artist. Three talented artists in one family—it's hard to imagine. Can you picture Al Hirschfeld with two equally gifted sons?

"Oscar Wilde" by Ape (Carlo Pellegrini).

The French

Charles Philipon was a minor artist but a major entrepreneur of caricature. He published the paper *La Caricature*, and later *Le Charivari*, which gave birth to the careers of Honoré Daumier, Traviès, Gavarni, Henri Monnier, Grandville and other Bohemian artists, including a sixteen-year-old Gustave Doré. A *charivari*, incidentally, is nothing but a shivaree, a noisy, clamorous parade. So here was a group of boisterous artists making rude noises and thumbing their comic noses at the new king, Louis Philippe. They were called by many "the demolishers of the bourgeoisie." When Louis Philippe ascended to the throne in 1830, following the July Revolution, his first act was to declare freedom of the press. Poor Louis Philippe didn't know what he was starting; it was a decision he would live to regret. He was responsible for putting into motion the richest, most fertile time in the history of caricature.

Philipon took this proverbial inch plus another mile when he and fellow artists began to attack the king. Philipon said "caricature shall henceforth be truth," and they went for the jugular. These artists were the first proponents of the *portrait-charge* (like the *ritratto carico*, a "loaded" portrait), and soon learned the power of caricature as a political weapon. Philipon became famous for depicting Louis Philippe as an obese pear. The king lost patience with these artistic, left-wing upstarts and soon put them all in prison. William Makepeace Thackeray, who himself dallied with caricature, commented that "the Press was sent to prison and

**"Croquades" by Charles Philipon:
the famous *poire*.**

as for poor dear Caricature, it was fairly murdered." Thackeray wrote an account of Philipon's trial that did little to restore to the king his damaged dignity.

The king accused Philipon of seditious libel and stated furthermore that these drawings were far from the *capriccio*, the whimsical creation, that Philipon contended: They were, in fact, bordering on treason. *La Poire* (which also means fathead or dullard in French slang) had become such a popular and easily drawn symbol that even schoolchildren were capable of scrawling that familiar shape on walls, thus further enraging His Majesty.

At his trial, Philipon produced a series of four sketches in his own defense. The first was an accurate portrait of the king. "This sketch," commented Philipon, "resembles Louis Philippe. Do you condemn it?" He then held up a second drawing of the king in which his outline began faintly to resemble a pear. The third drawing was clearly of a pear, which however bore a strong resemblance to the king. As he held up the last sketch, of a large Burgundy pear, he concluded, "If you are consistent, gentlemen, you cannot acquit this sketch either, for it certainly resembles the other three." In spite of this bit of courtroom theatrics, Philipon was found guilty and fined. Ultimately Philipon was forced to knuckle under to the wishes of the king and the pear became too expensive a symbol. The pear was thenceforth "exiled from the empire of caricature." After an attempt on his life in September, 1835, Louis Philippe found it expedient to blame the "anarchistic climate" that Philipon and his band of cunning caricaturists had helped to produce. Poor Louis Philippe, he tried to squash the efforts of these audacious artists only to see Philipon's new publication *Le Charivari* attain new heights of popularity. And for his efforts he is still remembered as—a pear.

One of *La Caricature*'s finest and most prolific artists was Honoré Daumier, who even today is remembered for his prints and drawings rather than his naturalistic paintings. Largely self-taught, Daumier exposed the faults of contemporary bourgeois society, as well as corruption in government, business and the courts, in his often scathing graphic works. When *La Caricature* was forced to close its modest doors because of additional pressure from the king, Philipon immediately established another paper, *Le Charivari*. Daumier worked on this paper for several years with a young writer named Honoré de Balzac, who once remarked of Daumier: "This boy has some Michelangelo under his skin."

One of *La Caricature*'s finest artists was Honoré Daumier, whose fine skills as a caricaturist all but eclipsed his image as a painter. Even today, Daumier is thought of as one of the truly great caricaturists, while his "serious" works go largely unnoticed. Daumier's cartoon of Louis Philippe as Gargantua, swallowing bags of gold belonging to his subjects, brought the king to imprison the artist for six months.

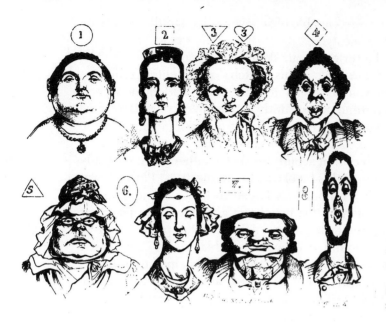

Grandville (Jean Ignace Isidore Gérard) was also a major contributor to *La Caricature* and *Le Charivari*. Here he offers us a wry lesson utilizing a series of head shapes.

Charles Joseph Traviès de Villers lived from 1804 to 1859, and was better known to the readers of Philipon's magazines as Traviès. After King Louis Philippe had all but banned humorous art from the press, the artists were forced to seek out less identifiable characters to speak for them. Traviès created a comical dwarf as the embodiment of humankind's weaknesses, and named him Mayeux. This warped character captured the public's fancy, as well as the attention of Victor Hugo, who used Mayeux as the inspiration for Quasimodo in *The Hunchback of Notre Dame*.

André Gill helped to popularize the *portrait-charge,* the unique approach developed by the artists of Philipon's *Le Charivari.* To be caricatured by Gill was an honor many sought; but Napoleon III was not amused when he was portrayed in a less than flattering light and saw fit to ban *La Lune,* the magazine for which Gill worked. The government became so paranoid about Gill's drawings that it went so far as to prevent publication of one of Gill's drawings of a cantaloupe, afraid that there might be contained in this drawing some sinister hidden meaning. Gill denied this to no avail; the government censored the cantaloupe. Here is his "Wagner."

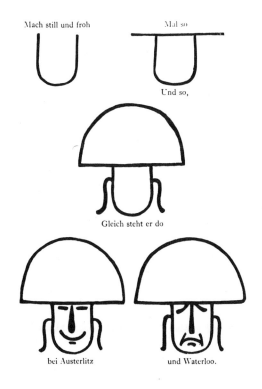

Mach still und froh

Mal so

Und so,

Gleich steht er do

bei Austerlitz

und Waterloo.

Wilhelm Busch enjoyed working in sequential panels to express movement or change. He began with abstract doodles and gradually developed them into recognizable figures. When he joined the staff of the Munich weekly *Fliegende Blätter,* and later the *Münchener Bilderbogen,* he developed the picture story, the precursor of our modern comic strips. He created a pair of popular characters named Max and Moritz in 1859. William Randolph Hearst was quite taken with them. He put Rudolf Dirks, a young staff cartoonist, on the project, and so two of America's most popular and enduring comic strip characters were born: Hans and Fritz of *The Katzenjammer Kids.*

C. R. Ashbee in his fine book *Caricature* offers us a loose translation of Busch's "Napoleon": "Make clean and pat/First this, then that:/Next add this too—/Here's Austerlitz,/There's Waterloo."

The Americans

America had not yet formed its standards of beauty when American caricaturists were starting to emerge, and consequently distortion was incomprehensible. Most American caricaturists did not exaggerate so much as they represented. Serious art was still the order of the day.

Although Paul Revere, a silversmith and engraver, is credited with many caricatures, history has proved him an imitator rather than a creator. Most of the drawings attributed to him were discovered in earlier versions in London magazines.

So that leaves Benjamin Franklin to wear the mantle of the first real American caricaturist. Franklin reveled in humor; his first and last published pieces were satirical. History confirms that he had a fine hand and was personally responsible for the drawings attributed to him.

During the Civil War, caricaturists, who for the most part represented the conservative, right-wing element, were guilty of the worst kind of blatant racism. Blacks were pictured as childish fools; Orientals, Jews and Catholics alike were reduced to ugly, ignorant stereotypes. Womens' rights advocates suffered the same fate at the hands of the nation's newspaper cartoonists. It wasn't really until Senator Joe McCarthy reared his controversial head that the political cartoonist/ caricaturist adopted a more liberal posture and moved to support civil liberties. Well, if nothing else "Tailgunner Joe" accomplished that much.

Few will deny that Thomas Nast was the most powerful, persuasive, doggedly

This caricature designed by Benjamin Franklin in London in 1774 represents Brittania after her limbs (representing the colonies) have been severed from her body.

Franklin's most famous caricature (the word for the political cartoons of that period) was rendered in 1754 at the beginning of the French and Indian War. This drawing, which urged the colonies to unite against a common foe, became a widely distributed handbill in 1776 and was subsequently often used as a newspaper heading.

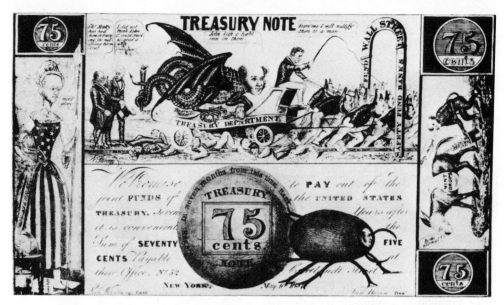

This complicated lithograph, done in 1837 by Napoleon Sarony, pictures the newly installed Martin Van Buren riding atop a wagon with a sign reading "Treasury Department." Van Buren is portrayed as a dragon shouting orders to his son John in the driver's seat, while the wagon runs relentlessly over a group of men. What makes this lithograph all the more remarkable are not just the political astuteness of the artist and his obvious draftsmanship, but the fact that Sarony was only fifteen years old when he produced this fine piece of work. But, of course, he had the advantage of never having seen a TV set or a video game.

determined caricaturist of all time. His daily attacks on William "Boss" Tweed and the Tammany Hall Ring are legend in the annals of caricature. German-born Nast was originally hired as a battlefield illustrator, but he aspired to say something with his sketches that would strike at the heart of the Civil War. His fame was instantaneous when "Compromise With the South" was published. The Republican Party circulated a million copies of Nast's drawing, and it ultimately became a potent force in the reelection of Lincoln in 1864.

Nast's star really soared when he took his instruments in hand (Nast preferred wood engraving to the comparative ease of lithography) and went after "Boss" Tweed and the political machine under his control. The Ring was consistently and blatantly robbing the city of New York. It had the gall to charge the city $2,870,464.06 for the services of one plasterer—for one month. (And we complained about Watergate!) Nast's brilliantly brutal cartoons, fifty in all, published in *Harper's Weekly*, eventually brought the "Boss" and the Ring to their knees and even helped triple the readership of the magazine . . . and Nast was still in his twenties.

Denis Tilden Lynch, in *"Boss" Tweed* (Boni and Liverwright, New York, 1927), tells about the time that Nast was visited by an officer of the Broadway Bank, not surprisingly a bank that Tweed had dealings with. After a few feeble conversa-

Thomas Nast's "Tweed-le-dee and Tilden-dum."

Nast is the artist responsible for the image of Santa Claus as we know it today; before Nast's version, Santa was leaner and sported a dark beard.

tional feelers, the man came to the point—he offered Nast a half million dollars in gold to back away from the anti-Tweed campaign and leave the country. Nast, of course, refused, and it wasn't long afterward that Tweed and his famous Ring got their well-deserved comeuppance. An ironic addendum to the Nast–Tweed tale: When Tweed was ousted from office, he fled to Spain and was subsequently spotted by someone who recognized him from a Nast caricature in *Harper's Weekly*. He was swiftly apprehended and returned to the United States, where he spent the rest of his days in a New York jail. When he died, among his effects was discovered every single cartoon that Nast had done of him—save the one that sent him to prison.

Nast has also received credit for creating the Tammany tiger, the Republican elephant and the Democratic donkey. He was, in fact, the father of all these except the donkey, which had already made a few appearances before Nast's career got underway. The Democratic symbol was originally a rooster, while the Whigs used a coon. The donkey at that time represented the Copperheads, Northern Democrats who opposed the Civil War.

Nast's skills were felt in many political arenas. After being elected President in 1868, Ulysses S. Grant is supposed to have said, "Two things elected me: the sword of Sheridan and the pencil of Nast." Nast launched a cartoon campaign

Frank Bellew drew this picture of Lincoln when he was reelected in 1864 and provided the caption "Long Abraham a Little Longer." Charles Dickens was a great admirer of Bellew's work; he wrote: "Frank Bellew's pencil is extraordinary. He probably originated more of a purely comic nature than all the rest of his brethren put together."

against Horace Greeley, of "Go West, young man" fame. Greeley had left his position as editor of the New York paper *The Tribune* after being nominated by both the Democratic and Liberal Republican parties for President. Nast's cartoons pictured Greeley dancing to the tune of Whitelaw Reid, the man who succeeded him as editor. Greeley died shortly after losing the election, and many people chose to believe that Nast's relentless attacks were partially responsible for his death.

Abraham Lincoln is revered as a legendary, almost Christlike figure in America: strong, wise, benevolent, not unlike the impressive marble statue that sits contemplatively in the Lincoln Memorial. That has not always been the case. When Lincoln first rose to power, he was treated badly by the press, especially the caricaturists. Lincoln was usually pictured as "a bearded ruffian, vulgar charlatan

Oddly enough, when Lincoln was assassinated, Sir John Tenniel, the caricaturist of the London *Punch,* was the first to do an emotional about-face when he drew a touching "Brittania Lays a Wreath on Lincoln's Bier." Notice the unchained slave at Lincoln's side.

Lincoln was pictured in a wide variety of ways: as an ugly child playing with his latest "toy," a new doll representing the latest in his long list of generals; as the federal phoenix rising from the ashes of the flaming Bill of Rights; or even, as pictured here, a paranoiac peering cautiously out of his boxcar. This cartoon by Adalbert Volck was, ironically enough, based on a rumor that Lincoln had disguised himself as a Scotsman (hence the tam-o'-shanter), fearing assassination while passing through Baltimore.

and repulsive beast." The attacks on Lincoln fell just short of out-and-out slander. Though it's hard to imagine today, Lincoln was a most hated figure during the Civil War. He was vilified, ridiculed, scorned and tormented. Sir John Tenniel, artist of the London *Punch,* was one of Lincoln's harshest critics, and supplied several of the inflammatory anti-Lincoln cartoons that appeared in the magazine between 1861 and 1865.

Lincoln did not take umbrage to the grave insults or the milder raillery (an apt word in his case) at his expense. He did not seem to mind being the butt of these cruel cartoons and actually seemed to enjoy them. Lincoln had great admiration for the visual arts and once called Thomas Nast "our best recruiting sergeant." Nast, who was most directly responsible for the image of Uncle Sam as we know him today, took his inspiration from Lincoln's craggy face and lean, scarecrowish body. The chin whiskers were added at a later date by Joseph Keppler, another prominent American caricaturist.

Before the advent of photography in the mid-1800s, the average citizen in the United States and elsewhere had only formal portraiture and/or caricature as a means to identify his or her illustrious or heinous leaders. The odds of the common people seeing their king, dictator or whatever in the flesh were slim indeed, so

Homer Calvin Davenport had the honor of being the highest-paid political cartoonist of his time. He had a winning way with a pencil and produced a series of devastatingly comic portraits for William Randolph Hearst's *New York Evening Journal.* Here was an artist that fired broadsides at his victims; no delicate épée thrust here. Davenport was a street brawler in terms of his work. His unrelenting caricatures of Mark Hanna, a Cleveland industrialist, pictured Hanna as an overweight rogue; these helped to steer public sentiment into the camp opposing Hanna and eventually caused New York state officials to propose an anti-cartoon bill in the state legislature. (To the utter relief of artistic freedom the bill was defeated.) After the 1896 election, Davenport and Hanna reportedly met and Hanna was heard to remark, "I admire your execution, but damn your conception." Davenport then published a drawing showing Hanna as he is and as Davenport made him, a drawing that could very well serve as a lesson in the art of caricature.

MARK HANNA AS HE IS AND AS DAVENPORT MADE HIM.

Strangely enough, Davenport's best-known drawing is humorless and rather tame compared to his usual standard. It proved, however, to be an effective campaign poster. The Republican Party shelled out nearly a quarter of a million dollars to circulate this piece for the election of 1904.

'He's Good Enough for Me!'

The same drawing appeared about twenty-eight years later, and helped to elect Franklin Delano Roosevelt. One of Hearst's staff artists switched heads and made the body considerably slimmer, and once again Davenport helped elect a President.

perceptions were based largely on artworks of the time. But then, which view to believe . . . the stiffly-posed, flattering portraits churned out by painters eager for their next commission, or the cruel caricatures distributed by opposing political factions? I opt for the caricatures—maybe it's the cynic in me. They are, in my opinion, a stingingly accurate record of the times and the people.

In a way, caricaturists then had an easier time of it (if we forget the cruel punishment they often suffered for their art); the common people were less demanding, and their ignorance of their leaders' faces made the artist's task a little simpler. Who could argue that the artist missed the nose but captured the expression in the eyes? Today we have the relentlessly intrusive medium of television to reveal to us every flaw, every enlarged pore on the faces of our idols and leaders— so the caricaturist's work is cut out for him. He must satisfy an extremely critical public, one better informed than has ever existed before. The caricaturist of today must become a brilliant stylist and delineator, or he must shift gears to the other extreme and annihilate his victims with bizarre artistic hyperbole.

When artists were faced with competing against the exacting eye of the camera, they were forced to move ahead into imaginative worlds where the camera could

Gustave Brandt's "Theodore Roosevelt—President of the United States." Teddy Roosevelt arrived tailor-made for caricaturists. They had a field day with his glasses, bushy mustache and wide toothy smile. He once said that the dentist was kinder to his teeth than the caricaturists were.

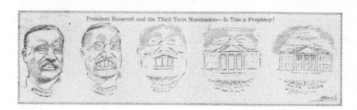

DRAWING
THE LINE
IN MISSISSIPPI

If Teddy hadn't gone on a bear hunt in Mississippi, we might never have had one of our favorite and most enduring toys. When the President refused to shoot a bear cub, he not only won the hearts of the American people, but inspired Clifford Berryman, a popular cartoonist, to create the "Teddy Bear."

not follow. The camera was in a sense the best thing that ever happened to art; it freed the artist from the bounds of formal realism and allowed his imagination to flower. The lens has a logistical point of view, but little else. The photographer can use a lens to distort and can play darkroom tricks, but nothing can match the ingenuity of the creative human mind. The camera has no opinion. Photography has so acquainted the average person with the famous faces of the day that the caricaturist is able to deal with the subtleties of the face; the humor is consequently less obvious and heavy-handed. At one time perceived as a grave threat to caricature, photography has actually served to enhance it.

Female caricaturists are decidedly conspicuous by their absence from these pages, but historically women were not encouraged to get involved in the arts . . . especially the humorous arts. Peggy Bacon, a prolific artist of the 1930s, was among the most successful women caricaturists. Her swift satires graced the pages of popular magazines, her book *Off With Their Heads* was a smashing success in its time.

Few other women have distinguished themselves in the world of caricature, or even in cartooning for that matter. Eva Herrman, Nell Brinkley, Grace C. Drayton, and Martha Orr are a few who rose to prominence in the early 1900s through the 1930s. Helen Hokinson was one of the first cartoonists hired by the *New Yorker* the year of its inception, and she subsequently designed nearly 2000 cartoons for that prestigious publication.

When William Howard Taft left office, the caricaturists were truly crestfallen. They had had tremendous fun at the expense of his girth and handlebar mustache. Oliver Herford, author of this caricature, was inspired to write:

"I'm sorry William Taft is out
Of politics; without a doubt
Of all the Presidential crew
He was the easiest to do."

A few decades later, another poet rewrote Herford's verse and came up with this gem:

"I'm glad that Gerald Ford is gone
He had a face more like a yawn.
I took my pen in hand to try for
Years to catch that facial cipher.
But now a brand new face appears
With hair, a grin, with teeth and ears.
I don't care if he's capable or understands the law,
I'll vote for the guy anytime that's easier to draw.

In 1935 *Little Lulu* was created as a *Saturday Evening Post* feature by Marjorie Henderson, a.k.a. Marge. Hilda Terry gave birth to *Teena* in 1941, the same year that Tarpe Mills came up with *Miss Fury,* an adventure strip.

Today we have France's Claire Bretécher and her fine satirical cartoons *Les Frustrés,* and of course Cathy Guisewhite's charming strip *Cathy.* The reason for the dearth of distaff caricaturists may best be summed up in the following story: Dale Messick, who created the popular Brenda Starr, red-headed reporter, tried for several years to peddle her ideas and met with rejection after rejection. At that time she was using her real name Dalia Messick. But when Dalia used the more masculine "Dale," *Brenda Starr* was accepted and soon became a staple comic strip in the households of America. Need I say more?

World War II provided the caricaturist with a whole new gallery of colorful characters, and soon the covers of *Collier's, The Saturday Evening Post* and other popular magazines were featuring horrifically comical portrayals of the Axis leaders. Hitler became the most caricatured person in history, deposing Napoleon from his spot on that dubious throne; Tojo was depicted as a sneaky, toothy dwarf, while Mussolini was pictured as an overweight, posturing fool. Historically, caricature has worked hand in hand with propaganda and has been one of its most effective and vicious tools, but never was the collaboration more keenly felt than during that dark period in the world's history. These heinous villains, vaingloriously bedecked with medals and badges, were fodder for the caricaturist's pen.

"Der Fuehrer's Face."
Copyright © 1942 Walt
Disney Productions.

You may notice the absence of caricatures during the Vietnamese war. But then, whom were we to caricature? Who was the enemy? He was a vague, faceless threat shrouded in controversy. And how does one draw the North Vietnamese ("the bad guys") as opposed to the South Vietnamese ("the good guys"), save that clumsy device of affixing labels to their clothing telling us who they are or where they're from?

Propaganda has been aptly defined as "the making of deliberately one-sided statements to a mass audience." And what better device than caricature? No better foils ever existed than the big three: Hitler, Tojo and Mussolini. Goebbels, Himmler, Hess and Goering were also exploited but they couldn't compare to that unholy trinity. It was wonderful for the United States. We could comfortably direct all of our hatred toward these three incarnations of malevolence. Even the usually apolitical world of the animated cartoon got behind the war effort. The normally innocent, fanciful Disney studios offered a cartoon short called "Der Fuehrer's Face" that enjoyed immense popularity. It featured Donald Duck as a reluctant assembly-line worker in the land of the Nazis.

Warner Brothers' cartoon studio, under the able guidance of Norman McCabe, turned out a flock of anti-Axis cartoons designed to impress even further our children's perceptions of our enemies: "Tokio Jokio," "Confusions of a Nutsy Spy," "The Ducktators" and even—you can't get any plainer than this—"Bugs Bunny Nips the Nips."

Warner Brothers turned to caricature in a big way during the 1940s; they used it as in-house advertising for their stable of working stars. It wasn't unusual to see "Malibu Beach Party," "Hollywood Canine Canteen," "Porky's Preview" or "A Star is Hatched" filled with the distorted cartoon visages of Bette Davis, Jack Benny, Edward G. Robinson and other Warner Brothers personalities.

If you think that the propaganda machine has ground to a halt, or that today's audiences are too sophisticated to be swayed by comic drawings, just think back to the investigation of the Watergate affair—a caricaturist's field day, where Nixon may have succeeded in dethroning Hitler as the most caricatured person of all time—or about the spate of drawings of the Ayatollah Khomeini during the Iranian hostage crisis. We were all emotionally manipulated day after day by the caricatures and cartoons we saw in our daily newspapers. Our prejudices were being neatly rearranged for us.

When Richard Milhous Nixon emerged as a political figure, the caricaturists must have jumped for joy. They were as ecstatic about Nixon's arrival as their forerunners had been disappointed at William Howard Taft's exit from public life—for a similar selfish reason. Nixon's jowly, heavy-browed countenance was a pleasure to draw. His hunched shoulders, strained smile and fingers shaped in a V were grist for the artist's mill. One of the first telling caricatures of Nixon was provided by Herblock in the *Washington Post* in 1954. Entitled "Here He Comes Now," it shows Nixon making an entrance from a sewer. It had a devastating effect

"Rose Mary's Baby" (Richard Nixon and Rose Mary Woods) by Richard Hess. Reprinted by permission of Richard Hess from *New York* magazine. Copyright © 1974 by Richard Hess.

"Eggheads." The Kennedy administration was not exempt from the barbs of the caricaturist. Here is a wry, pithy illustration by Robert Pryor, a frequent contributor to *Saturday Review, The New York Times, Harper's, Time,* and *Psychology Today.*

on Nixon; when he was running on the Republican ticket, he supposedly groaned, "I have to erase the Herblock image."

Watergate may very well be the most caricatured event in the world's history. In all fairness, we now have a broader media network, but still it is the champ. Nixon's face, in one awful distortion or another, greeted us every morning from the editorial page (helping to make him, incidentally, the most hated man in the world . . . at least according to Madame Tussaud's Wax Museum in London).

Many magazine and comic strip artists have employed caricature in their work. Peter Arno, the witty, suave contributor to the *New Yorker*, had a winning way with the faces of the celebrated. Walt Kelly, the creator of the comic strip *Pogo*, often invented characters that were dead ringers for the newsmakers of the day; one character with heavy brows and a dark smear of a beard bore an incredible resemblance to Senator Joe McCarthy. In his book *Equal Time for Pogo*, Kelly used Nixon, Lyndon Johnson, Hubert Humphrey and others as the basis for animal characters and deftly wove them into his satiric tapestry. Al Capp also utilized caricature in his popular *Li'l Abner* strip. In fact, he even went so far as to caricature a cartoon when he introduced Fearless Fosdick, an obvious satire on Dick Tracy. Jules Feiffer, the gifted artist, writer and playwright, has used caricature as a successful tool in his work. Aside from exposing the foibles and flaws of middle-class America, Feiffer has made frequent raids on our political community. He once commented, "Outside of basic intelligence there is nothing more important to a good political cartoonist than ill will." When Patrick Oliphant, the Pulitzer Prize-winning caricaturist and political cartoonist, was working on staff at the *Washington Star* and relentlessly jabbing some of the current jingoists, Art Buchwald said, "If I was in the White House, I'd lock him up and throw away the key." From a caricaturist's point of view, high praise indeed.

Sam Yorty, former mayor of Los Angeles, was skillfully skewered in 1968 by Paul Conrad, another Pulitzer Prize-winning cartoonist. The reactionary Yorty was making a shamelessly blatant bid for the post of Secretary of Defense with the Nixon administration. Conrad depicted Yorty as a nut case being humored by men in white coats. Yorty got indignant enough to sue the *Los Angeles Times* for two million dollars. The case was thrown out of court.

Conrad also turned out a series of devastating cartoons and caricatures of Richard Nixon. The highest compliment paid to the artist, according to him, was his being placed on Nixon's "enemies list." Conrad felt that at last he had arrived.

Fred Hartley, the Union Oil Company chairman, also took umbrage to a Conrad cartoon and sued for libel to the tune of four million dollars. He, too, lost.

A group of San Francisco artists launched a cartoon campaign against certain members of the California state legislature that was so intense that finally the injured parties outlawed caricatures that reflected on "a person's character and the publication of any portraits without the consent of the subjects." The laws were savagely ridiculed by the press and the public, and were ultimately repealed.

Anti-cartoon bills have also been attempted several times in Indiana, New York and Alabama. Fortunately they have all suffered the same fate.

Sardi's restaurant in Manhattan has been one of the show business crowd's favorite watering holes and dining places since the 1920s, and it's still going strong. It has a warm ambience, fine food and (not incidentally) hundreds of caricatures of the elite of Broadway and Hollywood gracing its walls. Four artists are credited with the drawings: Alex Gard began sketching the famous folks in 1929 and continued until his death in 1946. John Mackey took over for a brief time and added some twenty caricatures before he was relieved by Don Bevan. Bevan held sway over the empire until 1973, when he became a permanent resident of California. Since then, Richard Baratz has been the in-house artist for the more recent arrivals in the single largest public display of celebrity caricatures in the world. Here you see Skitch Henderson, Jayne Meadows and Steve Allen sitting below their respective caricatures. Reprinted by permission of Vincent Sardi, Jr.

The Amateurs

Caricature is one of those arts that nearly everyone—great and near-great alike—takes a crack at now and then. Many prominent people have enjoyed "the art of making faces on paper." Teddy Roosevelt was a frustrated cartoonist, and filled notepad upon notepad with his doodles. Sir Joshua Reynolds, the distinguished painter, was a wonderful caricaturist, as was Cecil Beaton, the famed photographer and theatrical designer. Jean Cocteau, the writer and film director, turned out many imaginative line drawings. John Barrymore was a gifted artist, as was his brother Lionel, who leaned more towards etching seascapes.

Among the best-known and most prolific celebrity caricaturists was Enrico Caruso. His talent for the graphic arts was recognized even before his singing ability, and he drew for pleasure his entire life. Caruso never had a lesson in caricature drawing, but he had a wonderful knack for capturing the essence of his subjects. Whether it was he himself in one of his operatic roles, another musician or a statesman, Caruso undisputably had "the hand." Caruso became the permanent caricaturist for *La Follia*, the Italian newspaper in New York, but he flatly refused to accept any payment for his work. Joseph Pulitzer offered him $50,000 a year for a weekly cartoon, but Caruso declined. Once Caruso spied one of his caricatures of Woodrow Wilson in the window of a shop. Upon learning that it was selling for seventy-five dollars, he remarked with a grin, "That is good pay for work of ten minutes. Better we stop singing and draw."

Enrico Caruso's caricature of Woodrow Wilson. Reprinted from *Enrico Caruso: His Life and Death* by Dorothy Caruso by permission of Simon & Schuster. Copyright © 1945 by Dorothy Caruso; renewed © 1972 by Mrs. Jacqueline Ingraham Porter.

David Hemmings, the fine British actor and star of *Blow-Up* and *Islands in the Stream*, drew this charmingly perspicacious sketch of his friend writer-director-producer Tom Mankiewicz.

George Gershwin tried his hand at self-caricature and came up with this simple but recognizable effort. Reprinted by permission of the Theatre Collection of the Museum of the City of New York.

Xavier Cugat, the perennially popular Spanish-born bandleader and motion picture personality, has been turning out caricatures since the 1930s. Here are but a few of the distinctive paintings that line the walls of Casa Cugat, his Los Angeles restaurant.

Robert Culp, the versatile motion picture and television actor, is apparently as much at ease at a drawing board as he is on a movie set or stage. In fact, the first money he ever earned was as a cartoonist. Here's a drawing he did of himself at the tender age of fifteen, and a bold, fluid caricature of a fellow actor who appeared with Culp and Katharine Cornell in *The Prescott Proposals* at the Broadhurst Theatre in New York. Culp hastily sketched the actor backstage at his insistence, but when the man saw the drawing he became indignant and proceeded never to speak to Culp again. Some days you just can't win. Reprinted by permission of Robert Culp.

WILLIAM III.,
King of Prussia.

Mark Twain gave it a valiant try, but he was less than successful with this version of His Majesty "William III, King of Prussia" (actually Emperor William I of Germany).

69

Chuck McCann, the gifted actor-comedian-impressionist and puppeteer, is no mean hand with a pen himself. Here's his impression (he works only from memory) of Gleason, The Great One, as Reggie Van Gleason III. Chuck, an old friend of mine from the struggling days in New York, was recently the recipient of ACE, the National Cartoonists Society Award. Reprinted by permission of Chuck McCann.

Like many other actors, Robert Redford has proven himself to be very versatile. Not only has he become an Oscar-winning director, but he has proved himself as a caricaturist, as shown by this drawing he did of character actress Thelma Ritter when he was attending the American Academy of Dramatic Arts. Reprinted by permission of Robert Redford.

Alfred Hitchcock's self-caricature was the logo into which he moved to come to life each week on *Alfred Hitchcock Presents*. With the widespread exposure and endless reruns of the program, this drawing may well prove to be one of the most familiar caricatures in history. Reprinted by permission of MCA Publishing, a division of MCA, Inc. Copyright by Universal Pictures, a division of Universal City Studios, Inc. All rights reserved.

Like the Carracci, Bolognese painters of the sixteenth century who indulged in caricature to "lessen the tensions of high art" (reminding us once again that caricature is "low art"), many fine artists have ventured into this area with impressive, sometimes charming results. Goya, Monet and Toulouse-Lautrec were especially gifted in the humorous arts. After having been harassed by Pope Paul III's chamberlain to complete his work in the Sistine Chapel, Michelangelo got even by depicting the testy annoying official as Minos, a serpent-like judge of the Underworld, in the lower portion of the *Last Judgment*.

The Practitioners

Caricature has had its ups and downs; it has fallen in and out of public favor from decade to decade. The fever for comic art ran high in Europe in the mid-1800s, the most prolific period in the history of caricature, and in the United States interest peaked during the 1920s and 1930s. With the advent of World War II, however, this interest waned. The horrors produced by the Axis powers were enough for the world; it didn't need, nor could it handle, an additional diet of warped distortions on paper. The prison camps in Europe and Asia were turning out their own brand of living caricatures devoid of humor or humanity.

George Grosz, Otto Dix and Max Beckmann were harsh critics of injustice and corruption in post-World War I Germany and in particular of the new Nazi regime. They were part of a movement called the "New Objectivity" that had only one formal exhibition, in 1925. Their paintings and pen-and-ink drawings graphically depicted the horrors of war, voluptuary war profiteers and government corruption. Both Dix and Beckmann saw their careers all but destroyed by the Nazis, who refused to let them exhibit their work. Dix was jailed in 1939 for complicity in a plot to kill Hitler. Grosz's publishers were repeatedly sued, and the artist narrowly escaped imprisonment time and time again. When he fled to America Grosz turned his back on his earlier style and attempted to become a popular commercial painter. He failed miserably. After having freely used caricature as a constant tool in his earlier (and most impressive) works, Grosz wrote in his autobiography, "More than ever I relegate caricature to a minor position in art; I believe that the

Here's a charming sketch that Picasso did of his friend art dealer Frank Perls as he appeared in his cameo role as Père Tanguy in *Lust for Life,* the movie about Van Gogh. Frank Perls Archives.

I have been a fan of Charles Bragg's wild, whimsical paintings for years. I had the pleasure of meeting this incredibly gifted artist and was not in the least surprised to find him every bit as strange and funny as his drawings. He allowed me to reprint this fine pencil sketch of Victor Hugo, but not without having to listen to several outrageous stories first (a small price to pay). Reprinted by permission of Harry N. Abrams, Inc., from *The Absurd World of Charles Bragg* by Geoffrey Taylor. Copyright © 1980 by Charles Bragg.

During a recent visit to the Motion Picture Academy theater, I happened upon an exciting display of caricatures by an actor turned artist named Bob Harman. I was taken not only by the quantity of his work (he has caricatured every major *and* minor player from Hollywood's Golden Age), but by the consistently high quality of his work as well. Mr. Harman lives and teaches in northern New York state, where he claims to paint eighty-five percent of the time. Here he has captured Hepburn, Grant, Stewart and the rest of the cast of *The Philadelphia Story*. Reprinted by permission of Bob Harman.

Fans of *Mad* magazine will recognize the distinctively economic style of Mort Drucker. He is one of today's most prolific and finest caricaturists, and his work has the unique quality of being simultaneously kind and perceptive—no easy task. Copyright © 1983 by Mort Drucker.

times when it predominates are times of decay. Surely life and death are big subjects, not subjects for sarcasm and cheap jokes." After producing a series of unsuccessful seascapes, Grosz returned to Germany in 1959 and subsequently drank himself to death.

In the late 1960s, a new group of artists appeared, and with the help of the old guard, they began, like Sisyphus, to roll caricature back up to the top of the mountain where it belonged.

Al Hirschfeld has stood at the helm of the ship of caricature since the 1920s, gracefully guiding her through the pages of the *New York Times* theater section. His distinctive style has helped to capture, in a kind, humorous way, the celebrity elite of the Broadway stage and motion pictures. Brooks Atkinson, the *New York Times* theater critic, wrote of Hirschfeld's drawings, "If they were not so entertaining people would realize that they rank with . . . Toulouse-Lautrec, Cruikshank, Rowlandson and some of the friskier aspects of Hogarth."

Hirschfeld's description of drawing is as simple and uncluttered as his work. "You know, you invent a problem and you solve it, but it's a problem of your own making."

Hirschfeld, whose friends include the wittiest people in the world, has always been a devoted fan of the humorous arts. He writes, "I have a special love for

This poster for *The Projectionist*, a movie starring Chuck McCann, Rodney Dangerfield and Ina Balin was created by the late, great Al Kilgore, a superb caricaturist who never fully received the recognition he deserved. Reprinted by permission of Maglan Films Inc.

Edward Sorel, he of the acerbically keen mind, has exhibited at the Louvre and is a regular contributor to major magazines all over the world. His pen, dipped in comic irony, has deftly deflated the egos of the wealthy, the well-known, the wicked and the wise. From *Superpen* by Edward Sorel. Copyright © 1978 by Edward Sorel. Reprinted by permission of Random House, Inc.

Ben Shahn committed his entire artistic life to social protest, and he used caricature as an important tool in that struggle. His dry, flat drawings exerted enormous power, and today's caricaturists use similar techniques. His drawings and paintings of Sacco and Vanzetti are considered masterpieces. Shahn collaborated with Diego Rivera on a fresco for Rockefeller Center (unfortunately now destroyed) and even designed ballets for Jerome Robbins. Here is his "Edward R. Murrow Destroying the Dragon of Joe McCarthy." Copyright © 1983, Estate of Ben Shahn.

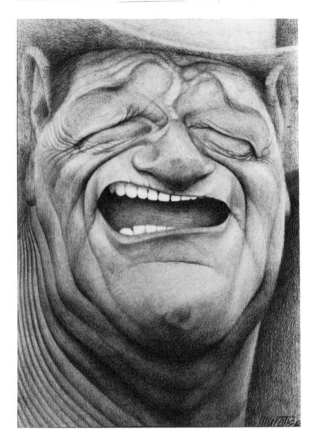

Jean Mulatier, Claude Morchoisne and Patrice Ricord are three Frenchmen who work out of the same studio in Paris. They have produced a series of incredibly popular *portraits-charge* of celebrities of today. Their techniques and style differ but they all adhere to an extremely high standard. One of their drawings can undergo thirty or forty preliminary sketches before it becomes a completed work—and even then, it sometimes takes three to four weeks. Here's Mulatier's wonderfully crafted caricature of John Wayne, portraying him in a respectful, loving light; a fine example of what Beerbohm called capturing the subject "at his most characteristic moment." You can almost hear Wayne's dry, flat readings emanating from that crooked mouth. Copyright © 1983 by Dervish Publications 1000.

Fons Van Woerkom's savage and outrageous cartoons have been enjoyed by the readers of the *Toronto Daily Star* and *The New York Times*. Dutch-born Fons's jaundiced view of the world is reflected in his brilliant yet often bitter drawings. Here is his perceptive Norman Mailer in *A Fire on the Moon*. From *Face to Face* by Fons Van Woerkom. Copyright © 1973 by Fons Van Woerkom. Reprinted by permission of Alfred A. Knopf, Inc.

humor, for wit. I always think that humorous writing is much more serious than so-called serious writing. It's more profound to me."

Ever since Hirschfeld's daughter Nina was born in 1945, he has cleverly woven her name into the tapestry of his work. A number follows his signature, prompting an army of Hirschfeld freaks to try to discover *Nina* hidden that many times in the swirls and flourishes that distinguish his drawings.

Superb artists like David Levine, Edward Sorel and Mort Drucker joined forces with Al Hirschfeld and others and revitalized the not dying, but definitely wounded, art. A renaissance of caricature in the United States is moving in direct correlation to the other comedic arts: Stand-up comedy has found a new audience, the humorous novel is making another bid for acceptance in the marketplace. I view all of these as positive signs of a sort of psychological recuperation. When we can laugh at ourselves, we are on the road to health and recovery. To silence those detractors who maintain that caricature is not alive and well and still kicking the stuffing out of things, I present samples of the work of some of these fine caricaturists.

Now that I have shown you the crème de la crème, the elite of the world of caricature, I have the unmitigated gall (or perhaps the lack of good sense) to try to instruct you, the aspiring caricaturist, in this peculiar and particular art. If you're game, I am. Read on.

The Technique

Drawing a caricature is something like the opposite of that old Johnny Mercer tune "Accentuate the Positive." But in caricature we accentuate the negative and often eliminate the positive altogether. We take a face and squash it, distend it, pull it, push it and still try to preserve its resemblance to the original.

Caricature requires, among other things, acute powers of observation. Sometimes this makes people nervous. After all, a burning gaze (you might be memorizing someone's face for a later sketch) is rather disquieting. Let me give you a few words of warning based on hard experience: Do not (I repeat, do *not*) caricature any member of your mate's family, unless you're fond of sleeping in the den, or unless you can, in all conscience, whip off one of those innocuous sketches that make the members of the clan look like refugees from a Disney storyboard. I don't have that ability; I head right for the jugular.

Another semi-sage suggestion: Never draw yourself looking better than anyone else, even if you do, in fact, look better; you will be placing yourself in a totally indefensible position. I'm not suggesting that self-caricature is easy—it's not. It's probably harder than drawing others, as we'll see later on in this chapter.

Mark Twain once said, "A man can't tell the truth until he's dead." He should have added "or unless he's a caricaturist." Truth is the goal of caricaturists; they stalk their prey, cutting through the charming smokescreen, and hone in on the truth beyond the artifice. The caricaturist seeks out the characteristic flaw: the close-set eyes, the crooked smile, the lantern jaw. In the hands of a caricaturist, the lean become skeletal, the chubby blossom into waddling whales, and a "generous" nose becomes, as Cyrano boomed, "a peninsula."

Another word of warning: Skill in caricature is not a passport to instant popularity, like playing the piano well. There are those stuffy folks out there who can't handle seeing themselves pictured in a less than flattering light. They love seeing others lampooned, but they have a blind spot when it comes to themselves. They beg off with a variety of lame excuses, the most common one in the form of a boast, "Well, of course, I'm very hard to do." To this kind of person, humerus is merely a bone in the arm.

So to be a caricaturist you must be observant, perceptive and truthful (see?—so far, I have not described a potentially popular person) *and* maybe have a little talent with a pencil. You'll notice I said a "little talent." Superior draftsmanship is useful, but not necessary to be a caricaturist. In the area of the *portrait-charge*, however, it's an indispensable prerequisite: That form lies somewhere between a portrait and an attempt to make the subject appear hideous. But not so in caricature. Max Beerbohm was not a great draftsman, but his wit and his gentle, unique vision helped to ensure him a well-deserved place in the ranks of the great caricaturists.

You certainly couldn't call me a trained artist. I have just been persistent enough to develop some drawing ability. I formulated my technique for caricature in a rather seat-of-the-pants, trial-and-error way, but it has helped me out of some sticky situations. It's nice to have a crutch to lean on when you're confronted with having to do one of the world's blandest faces, or when someone rushes up to you at a party, drink in hand, demanding, "Draw me! I just love characters!" (They mean "caricatures," but they haven't yet gotten the hang of the language.) Anyway, in these situations, I always do exactly the same thing—I panic. Or I used to; now I have a technique to depend on, and so far it hasn't let me down.

Though I'm not proud to admit it, I am a totally unschooled artist, and I certainly can't recommend the process by which I learned to draw. When I was a child, I would put my hand next to my eye, sight down my finger as though it were a rifle barrel and trace around things: trees, buildings, cars, people, whatever and wherever. . . . I did this in school, in church, everywhere—and all the time. More than once I heard passing strangers murmur fearfully, "Look at that crazy kid." After a while I learned to continue "sighting" and moving my hand away from my face to a piece of paper, and my drawing "technique" was born. Weird, but what would you expect from someone in my line of work?

If you are an insecure beginner, or an artist who has just never caught on to caricature, stay with me. This formula has worked pretty well for me; I hope it can do the same for you.

The technique involves the use of a "grid." Let me explain.

All of us carry around in our minds a mental grid, if you will, a template of the perfectly proportioned face, by which we measure and judge every face we see. A hundred times a day we automatically determine whether someone is beautiful, handsome, attractive, pretty, cute, homely, ugly or grotesque. The difference between beautiful and pretty or homely and ugly is only a matter of millimeters and yet we all generally agree on these subtle distinctions. This visual standard,

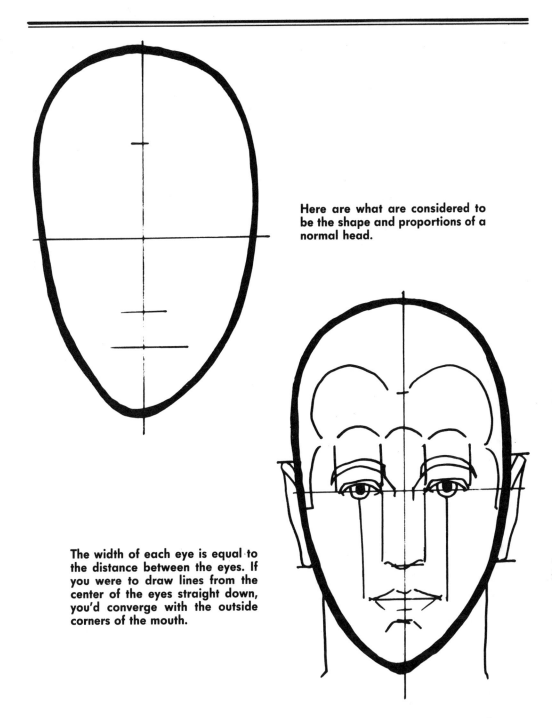

Here are what are considered to be the shape and proportions of a normal head.

The width of each eye is equal to the distance between the eyes. If you were to draw lines from the center of the eyes straight down, you'd converge with the outside corners of the mouth.

imposed upon us by our socio-cultural environment, is ever present and quite important to our lives. We learn our aesthetic preferences while very young. We are all taught to judge our fellow human beings quickly by the way they appear to us. Perhaps "ugliness" is the last major bastion of prejudice yet to be overcome.

Here are what are considered to be the shape and proportions of a normal head. You'll notice that the eyes cut the head in half horizontally. Halve the lower area horizontally for the mouth, and the upper section vertically for the eyes. The hairline is approximately halfway between the top of the head and the eyes, although this differs radically from face to face. The ears reach from the top of the eyebrows to the bottom of the nose.

The width of each eye is equal to the distance between the eyes. If you were to draw lines from the center of the eyes straight down, you'd converge with the outside corners of the mouth. People commonly have difficulty placing the ears in profile drawings; they either hang the ears way on the back of the head or set them on the cheeks, too close to the eyes. As the illustration shows, draw a right-angled triangle at the corner of the eye: One leg will extend to the jawline, and the other, of equal length, will extend to the outer edge of the ear.

The reason I stress these dimensions is that before we can corrupt, distort, bend, squash, pull, bulge, elongate or shorten, we must be acutely aware of the correct proportions. You can't exaggerate until you know the subtle inconsistencies in a face. Only by recognizing the "norm" are we qualified to move into the world of the "abnormal."

Using this grid technique, follow me as I take a group of faces, some celebrated, some not, and gradually turn them into caricatures by slowly distorting their features.

When I do a preliminary sketch, whether from life or photographs, I like to take notes about my impressions at the time. I've included them here in the hope that they will help you.

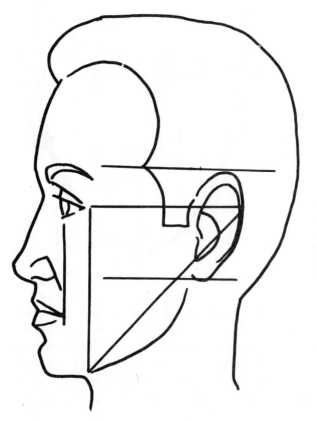

To place the ears in profile, draw a right-angled triangle at the corner of the eye: One leg will extend to the jawline, and the other, congruent leg will extend to the outer edge of the ear.

The problem of how to attack a subject is much like the decision a director must make on a movie set: where to put the camera? The caricaturist asks himself the same question: What best suits this face—profile, full face or three-quarter? Each angle makes its own separate statement. Do you want to see the body—is it important, does the body contribute to the subject's identity? Here I am stressing primarily facial caricature, but that is not to suggest that I'm detracting from the importance of the body. Again, it depends upon the subject matter: Fred Astaire, Bette Midler and Rudolf Nureyev have personas that are strongly associated with their bodies, whereas Dan Rather, Walter Cronkite and other "talking heads" can be captured just as effectively in strict facial caricature.

Do you want to depict your subject as smiling, sulky, moody, hysterical or placid? And why? Sometimes by choosing an uncharacteristic expression, you can make a wonderfully ironic statement about the person. A usually somber face becomes a comic mask when it's invaded by an uncommonly warm smile. And conversely, a grinning fool takes on another dimension when he's delineated as a serious-minded citizen. One of the pleasures of caricature is recognition, the other is shock. I once saw a magazine article whose premise was that Jesus Christ had a sense of humor and was not the pious, humorless man so often depicted in motion pictures and television shows. The illustration showed Jesus, his head thrown back, laughing uproariously. The point of all this is that the illustration was extremely eye-catching. I'm suggesting that the same thing can be accomplished with a caricature. Use surprise; it's a wonderful tool.

If you continue to draw and think and let your imagination run free, there are no limits to where it can take you. I was once having enormous difficulty with a drawing of Liberace: The resemblance was there, but there was no life, no "kicker" to take it out of the mundane and into the special. Then I hit upon an idea that turned the entire drawing around for me: Liberace appears grinning his sycophantic grin, his teeth transformed into a piano keyboard.

When you sit down at your drawing board or the kitchen table to do a caricature, the first thing to do is to assess the face clinically, measure its strengths and weaknesses and its neutral features. Is the head round, sloped or triangular? Are the brows bushy or sleek, or are they insignificant little commas? Do the ears belong on a 747, or do they cling tenaciously to the sides of the head? Once you have determined the relationship of one feature to the other, then it's time to go to work "re-orchestrating" the face. Lift a nose here, drag a jowl down there, add more meat to an already meaty face. By "neutral" features, I mean those that don't have a distinctive shape; if they don't make a valuable contribution to the face's character, they are neutral and can either be kept in relatively correct proportion or be eliminated entirely. Be ruthless; if they don't add anything, drop them.

And remember that a caricature isn't just an exaggeration of one or two features; the features should be in concert with one another. You could easily capture Bob Hope in a few lines because of his high celebrity status; you could get away with using just his famous ski-jump nose and be done with it. But why not include those mischievous eyes, that jaunty chin, cocky smile and slicked-back hair? They are all important ingredients in the overall recipe of his face.

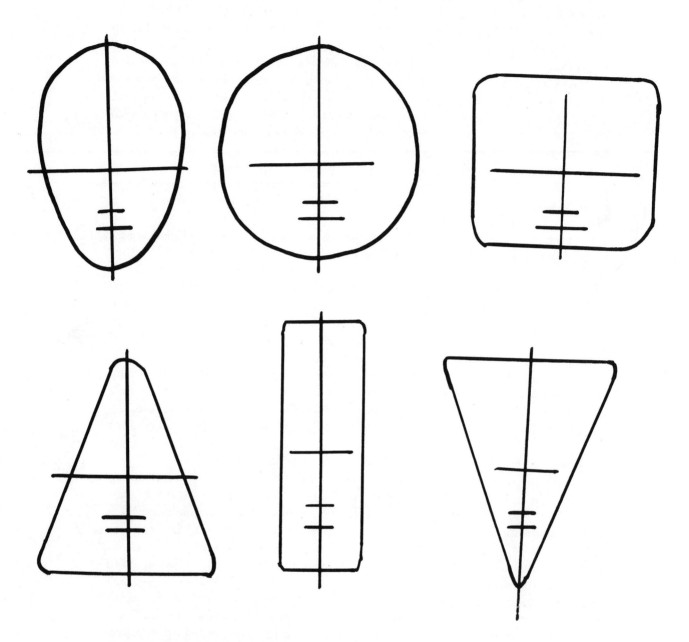

Here are the six basic head shapes that I like to work with: oval, round, square, pear shaped, rectangular and triangular. Most faces fall into these general categories, or combinations of them, i.e., an oval and a circle, or a square inside a triangle. When you look at someone, try to identify his or her head as one of these shapes.

Here are some familiar faces to give you an idea of how important the shape of the head can be.

Let's take a face and begin to shift the features around within the framework of the grid to achieve a caricature. Here's a sketch of producer-actor John Houseman. (You ask why I chose him in particular? Because he's not that hard to do— I'm no fool.)

I see Mr. Houseman's face as a square inside a triangle. If I'm satisfied that that's his basic head shape, I can start assessing the features individually.

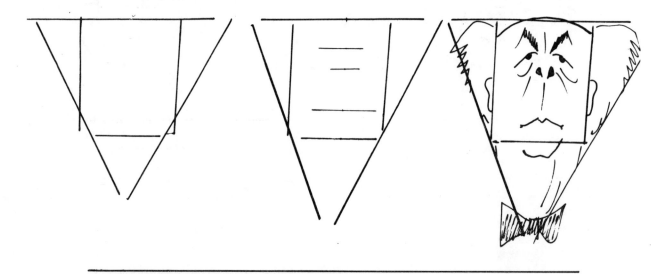

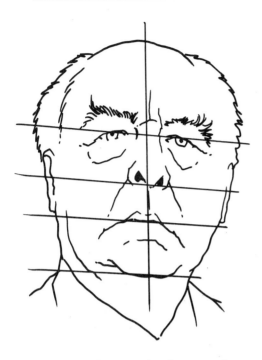

Houseman's nose is short, so I move the nose well above the eyeline.

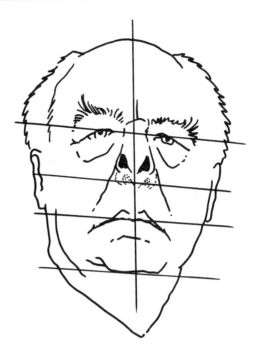

This automatically lengthens his upper lip, so I keep the mouth about where it is. I minimize the chin in order to accentuate the jowl and neck area. Look at the downward cast of his mouth and the arch of those brows that give him that haughty, imperious look.

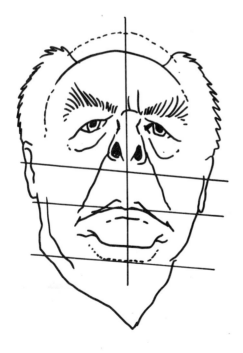

I exaggerate the angles of the eyes and mouth, making them droop downward; the eyebrows become Mephisthophelean.

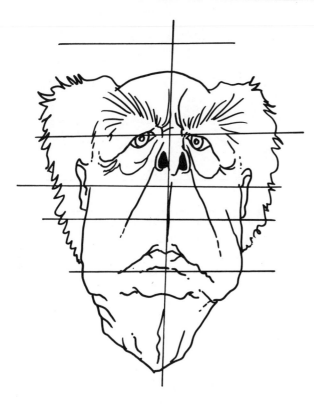

I reduce his pate and scramble up his hair to suggest a wild professorial look.

So you see, by shifting the elements, by exaggerating and minimizing, we've arrived at a fair resemblance.

Drawing human faces on animals or drawing humans to look like animals, as I mentioned before, is as old as antiquity. It is convenient for artists that we have invested nearly every animal with some human vice or virtue; the owl is wise, the fox is sly, etc. These shorthand symbols facilitate the "character" in caricature. We can all grasp these symbols immediately. One of the anthropomorphically imposed traits in the animal/man registers with us instantly, and the artist is already way ahead of the game.

If we go a few steps further with this caricature of Mr. Houseman, we can easily turn him into an owl (fitting because of the sage men he plays) . . . or even a dog. If this is done carefully, there's no reason why you can't retain the resemblance.

This man's friendly, open face . . .

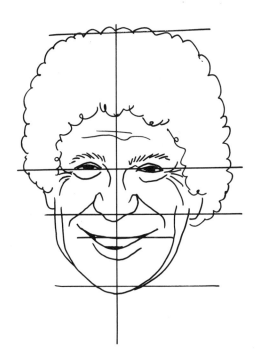

. . . is basically a circle inside an oval.

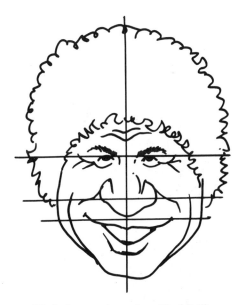

His hair turns into electrified Brillo; his small eyes all but disappear and cling fearfully to the bridge of his nose; his nose becomes a lump of kneaded clay.

Check the original grid against what we've ended up with; you can see how the proportions within the face have changed.

What strikes you most about this man's face?

His penetrating round eyes? His trim, firmly set mouth?

His hair like a beaver pelt, with straggly bangs?

Eyes like polished almonds. A sweetly curving mouth.

Hair like a wheat field. A saucy, ambitious nose.

Steady, inquisitive gaze.

Nostrils smelling something quite unpleasant. Firm, judgmental mouth.

Ears like undersized conch shells. Thin hair escaping from the face.

Tom Bosley (of *Happy Days*), an old friend of mine from Broadway, has a delightfully puckish attitude.

An ethnic leprechaun. Eyebrows in a constant state of childish wonder.

Cheeks like pincushions.

A narrow, proud nose. Eyes that confess a profoundly sad secret.

A thatch of unruly hair.

Cheeks like antique leather.

Here we have a sort of spoon-shaped head.

A dominant nose.

Remote, melancholy eyes with plunging eyebrows. A chin that aspires to be part of the neck.

Kind, dark eyes swimming in a mass of wrinkles.

Eyebrows like tiny gray explosions.

A corrugated brow leading up to hair like a snow trail.

The caricaturist cringes when a new face that is difficult to do appears on the public horizon. Ronald Reagan initially presented such a problem, but then the caricaturists got a handle on his flabby jowls and low hairline; now he's a snap. When Gerald Ford's bland physiognomy presented itself, caricaturists delivered a collective groan. As some wag once said, "A Gerald Ford makeup kit consists of an empty box." Ford was chagrined at the way he was treated by the press and newspaper cartoonists. At a viewing of a group of political cartoons, he was heard to sigh, "The pen is mightier than the politician."

The face that has some character, a set of interesting features, will long outlive the neutral pusses of this world. Teddy Roosevelt, with his mustache, glasses and exotic hats, will be remembered long after Calvin Coolidge's nonexistent physiognomy. The German painter Max Liebermann once said of a man with a totally forgettable face, "A face like his I can piss into snow."

One caricature, when reproduced in hundreds of thousands of copies, can act as an advertisement, and consequently certain physical props and idiosyncrasies become an inextricable part of the person. Elton John's glasses, Nixon's bushy-browed scowl, John Denver's haircut, FDR's cigarette holder have become so linked with these luminaries that the public comes to expect the inclusion of these symbols and is disappointed or confused if the artist fails to use them.

This is a mixed blessing for the artist; on the one hand he's aided by these shorthand symbols, and on the other his artistic imagination is stifled by them. The artist has to find a way not only to skirt the cliché, but also to satisfy his artistic integrity. I once did a drawing of Groucho Marx that I felt captured some of his

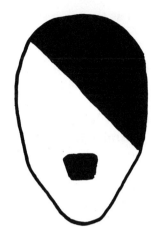

brazen irreverence, but friends of mine asked, "Where's the cigar? He always smokes a cigar." In their eyes I had failed to capture him. The cigar as a symbol had superseded the art.

When William Auerbach-Levy, the gentle theatrical caricaturist of the 1930s, was about to do Eugene O'Neill, he was urged by his friends to "be sure to do the large eyes." Auerbach-Levy, either to be contrary or to prove a point, went the other way and entirely omitted O'Neill's expressive eyes, and still produced a wonderful likeness.

Vocal impressionists, like John Byner and Fred Travalena, do with their voices what caricaturists do with their pens. The comedic point of view is the same, as is the distortion; both types of artists do not faithfully imitate so much as they offer us the flavor, the rhythm, the exaggerated essence of an individual. And our reaction is the same; we experience, as Auerbach-Levy said, "the pleasure of recognition."

Often what we're hearing is an impression of an impression. One especially sharp-eared performer has stumbled upon the elusive key to a voice and the others, most of their work already done for them, merely imitate the imitator. It has been boiled down to its essence for them.

Vocal and graphic caricatures are solidly connected. I was once attempting an impression of Clark Gable, but I couldn't catch his voice until I sat down and drew his furrowed brow, his pursed lips, his arrogant smile; then suddenly I was "inside" him and was able to do a passable impersonation. It was as though a secret key had turned.

The beginning caricaturist will inevitably ask the question, "How far should I go?" I say, go as far as the resemblance remains, go as far as your imagination tells you to go . . . within the bounds of good taste. Ay, there's the rub—that elusive ingredient, taste. Obviously the unfortunates among us, those who suffer from birth defects or other disfiguring ailments, are not fair game. And yet, how far is far? When does the ugly become grotesque and off limits to the caricaturist? W. C. Fields's nose was a large, bulbous mass of quivering flesh, yet since he himself made fun of this "protuberant proboscis," as he was fond of calling it, it was okay for others to do the same. The same applies to a myriad of celebrated people who have cashed in on their weaknesses for the sake of art, e.g., Bob Hope's ski-jump nose, Eddie Cantor's eyes, to name a couple.

The heinous villains of history can be made to look as hideous as we wish, and that is acceptable; the punishment fits the crime. But to make a grotesque out of someone who is only *accused* of a crime or to shamelessly ridicule a political figure with whom you disagree is to tread on dangerous ground. Take President Reagan for instance. If the artist were too blatantly savage in his attack, if he were to turn Reagan's neck folds into sagging, blubbery strands and reduce his already low hairline to simian proportions, he would risk an emotional backlash. The intent could very well backfire. Americans have a tendency to root for the underdog, because historically they fear power. If someone is attacked too viciously, this underdog syndrome could surface and the caricaturist's work would be all for naught. There is a parallel in nightclub entertainment, where I paid my dues for a few years. If a heckler disturbs the show with mild interruptions and the performer throws an arsenal of professional insults at him and all but destroys him, then the audience, which formerly resented the heckler, will turn its anger toward the performer. So my warning is this: Be cautious in the degree of ridicule; a little goes a long way.

William Auerbach-Levy, in his book *Is That Me?*, wrote, "Avoid over-exaggeration or you will defeat your aim. If you over-exaggerate you will miss the mark. You will succeed only in making your subject hideous instead of funny, and instead of laughter you would evoke only repugnance." Well, that was in the 1930s, and things have gotten wilder, looser and more outrageous since then. Gerald Scarfe's wild, uninhibited drawings rest on the brink of repugnance and yet they remain funny and, what's more, recognizable. They certainly make a more stinging commentary than Auerbach-Levy's gently taunting portraits.

So what is the answer? You must look into your heart finally for that, but remember what a nineteenth-century artist said: "A good caricature can only be appreciated by its victim." You can be kind or cruel, savage or satirical, but be truthful. Fire a BB gun or a broadside, but be fair. Use a needle or a cleaver, but be responsible. When truly homely people approach me for a caricature, I die a little inside. The decision is especially difficult: To represent them faithfully means to risk wounding them, and they've probably suffered enough because of their homeliness; to try to flatter them a bit and make them look a little better than they do smacks of condescension, and a sensitive person will spot it and possibly be even more wounded as a result. A caricaturist must on occasion be especially tactful, and I confess that I can't lay claim to that ability. Maybe this is why I'm reluctant to do caricatures in public.

Technique, like taste and style, is an elusive thing. It requires constant experimentation before you feel that "oneness" and ease that tell you you've found your medium. Caricature has been expressed in every medium from crayon to charcoal, from bronze to oil. I've tried to include a variety of techniques and approaches throughout this book so that you might find those that reach out to you and inspire you to continue.

My personal choices for media are very soft lead pencils, colored pencils, felt-tip pens, brushes and, on occasion, a big fat marking pen. They all have their own individual appeal to me and convey different feelings. I rarely do a soft, lovely woman with anything but pencil or pastel, because I can control the subtleties better with them. I save stronger, bolder implements for craggy, weatherworn faces. I like working with colored pens, which I smear around with the tip of my moistened finger. It produces interesting effects, including rainbow-colored fingertips. But beware—hard to remove, but a great ice-breaker at parties: "Why do you have multicolored fingertips?" And the conversation is off and running.

Being a basically lazy person, though I'm loath to admit it, I like working on vellum paper. Vellum is a very strong paper transparent enough to trace through; it comes in a variety of sizes and weights, and it can be found in any good art supply store. The advantage here is that if you make a drawing that you like, but there is an area you'd like to rework, you can trace through safely and preserve the integrity of your first sketch while making the desired changes.

I usually sketch a face ten to twenty times before I'm satisfied that the resemblance is strong enough to move on to the finished drawing. It is at this stage that I decide on the medium to be used. The finished sketch will tell me whether it should be done in ink, pencil, crayons or the "rainbow-finger" technique.

Often, if I've gotten too close to the drawing, I'll resort to the mirror trick that I use for self-caricature (see page 106) to get that fresh outlook on the work. Generally, I recommend going for the head shape first, zeroing in on that and then beginning to build the features in that area. Mort Drucker, the excellent caricaturist from *Mad* magazine, says, "We all have the same features, it's the space between them, their proportions and relationships to one another that distinguish one face from another. I let features swim around the facial area until I feel that they've been arranged properly and the spatial relationships are right."

I admit that I am by nature an eclectic; I like moving from technique to technique, although I'll be the first to disparage that approach. It's much better to find your personal style. Al Hirschfeld's drawings are instantly recognizable as his and no one else's; the same applies to David Levine, Edward Sorel and many others. We feel comfortable and secure seeing those familiar lines and curves. They've become a part of our subliminal world and we respond to them like old friends. So take my advice and find a style that doesn't wander; find that unique vision that lurks inside of you.

Here are two profile studies of W. Somerset Maugham. I chose this angle because of its wonderfully chiseled appeal. You should always let the subject's face dictate to you whether it should be done full face, three-quarters or profile. In the second sketch, I've pulled his nose and chin together with an invisible string, thus emphasizing his jutting chin and the downward cast of his mouth. It's a little like manipulating a rubbery hand puppet.

Here's something I've always wanted to see done with Hitler.

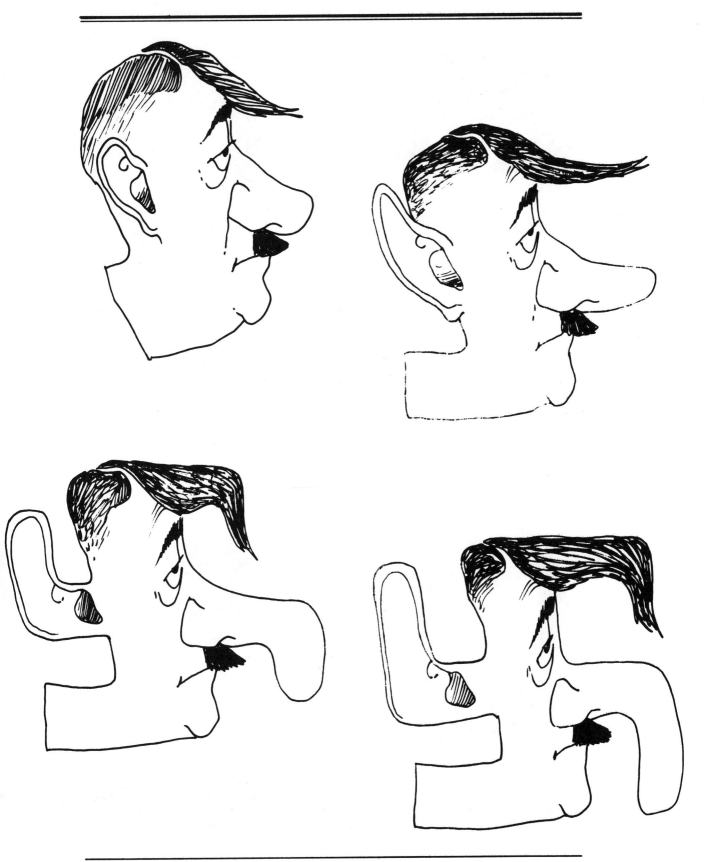

Saturnine eyebrows. A devilish grin. Even teeth.

Squinty, clever eyes. Neatly trimmed beard and hair.

With a little effort we can take this man's face further . . .

. . . to its "natural" conclusion: Here is the result of Lawrence Talbot's lunar metamorphosis. As you become more adept and more confident, you'll eventually be able to bypass the intermediate steps and zero right in on the key feature in the subject's face.

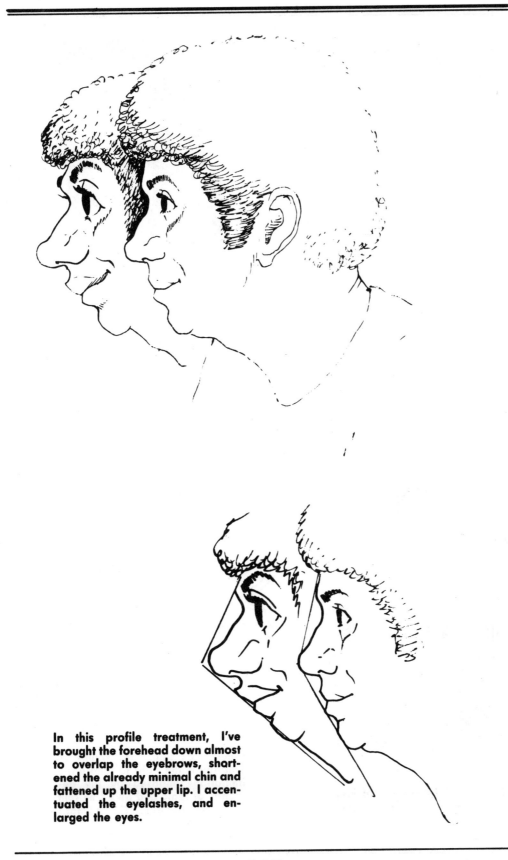

In this profile treatment, I've brought the forehead down almost to overlap the eyebrows, shortened the already minimal chin and fattened up the upper lip. I accentuated the eyelashes, and enlarged the eyes.

Bulging, assertive eyes.

Eyebrows arched dangerously.

A flat, broad forehead and hair that clings tenaciously to a sloping head.

Freud once said, "The whimsical creation is the right to ignore the limitations imposed by the demands of logic and give free rein to . . . imagination." This is what I tried to do here.

Pale, lost eyes. A comfortably soft nose.

Ears like eagles' wings and a mustache that could sweep a fireplace clean.

A friendly, discarded old shoe.

A quick word about style. First of all, it can't be taught. Style is that intangible special quality that each of us possesses as a result of our personal vision and unique life experience. I can, however, suggest in one word a way to find your style—draw. Draw constantly, incessantly, compulsively, draw. Soon your own distinctive flair that lies dormant inside of you, just waiting to be released, will emerge. Without urging or forcing or seeking, your style will make itself known. It will surface in spite of you if you will just draw. The more you take pencil in hand, the less labored each drawing becomes and the more you're able to relax. The more you relax and enjoy the drawing experience, the more your style is given free rein to express itself. There will always be a better draftsman, a finer painter, a superior technician, but no one can ever duplicate your style.

We are all influenced by other artists; we cannot help that. But there is a wide difference between subliminal influence and out-and-out imitation. Your style is your most precious gift. Never sacrifice it for the sake of expediency. Whatever your talents or limitations as an artist, never let the paper be aware of your insecurity. Your stroke should be bold and confident; commit to the line. The tentative pen has no place in caricature: a brave slash for the mouth, a swooping curve for the nose. Very often speed can help you to counteract timidity; it can, in a sense, force you to be sure.

Again, I know I have already stressed this a lot, but *draw*. It's the only way that you'll ever find that comfortable relationship between the pencil in your hand and the paper. Soon you'll be involved in the process of drawing, and your hand will seem to move without conscious guidance. Robert McKim, in *Thinking Visually,* says, "Drawing and thinking are frequently so simultaneous that the graphic image appears almost an organic extension of the mental processes." Edward Hill likens a drawing to a mirror: "A drawing acts as a reflection of the visual mind. On its surface we can probe, test and develop the workings of our peculiar vision." William Feaver, in *Masters of Caricature,* says that "caricature is the quickest of the arts and the most disconcerting." It's true, "the art of making faces on paper," as someone once called it, should be accomplished with apparently effortless ease. The trick is to conceal the craft and the effort.

Let's spend a moment talking about self-caricature, an area in which I've been eminently unsuccessful. We all think that we know what we look like, but we're usually a few light-years from the truth. That face that stares back at us from the bathroom mirror every morning has been graciously strained through our protective psyche.

My experience with drawing myself has been that my first attempts (if I dare show them to anyone) are met with indignant cries of "Hey, Dick, you're not *that* ugly!" My next sketch usually represents the opposite pole, for now I get pursed lips and a different reaction, "Come on, you think you're that cute, do you?" Again I skulk back to the drawing board for another try.

All I can suggest here, if you have as little self-objectivity as I do, is to draw from photographs of yourself. When you're done, hold the sketch up in front of a mirror and appraise the reflection you see. It gives you just that much more objectivity.

This also works when you've done a face too many times and are too close to your work. It offers you a quick, fresh outlook.

Back in the 70s I did a TV series called *When Things Were Rotten* for Mel Brooks. It was short-lived but fun; I played a wacky Robin Hood. I drew a caricature of our whole group, and included Mel as a benevolent sun shining down on his lads of Sherwood Forest. It wasn't bad; it made a few TV magazine covers around the country. I received a thank-you letter from Mel that said, "You did a nice job on the group caricature but how come you made yourself look like Snow White?" See what I mean? You have to be careful.

I hear many pro-and-con discussions about the best way to work—from life or from photographs. I don't see a big choice here: How many of us can call up Prince Charles or Ronald Reagan and ask either of them to sit for a caricature? Most of us are forced to work from photos.

Norman Rockwell wrote that "photographs are a great time saver and I don't know how I could get through my work without them."

William Feaver wrote that "the true caricaturist works mainly from memory and so keeps his impressions intact."

David Levine prefers to work from photographs, as he feels that the live subject could charm the artist into a kinder expression of him or her. The eminent British caricaturist David Low, on the other hand, once remarked that "doing a caricature from a photograph was akin to writing a biography from *Who's Who*." As the story goes, Low used to discreetly tail his subjects in order to catch candid glimpses of them.

Personally, I enjoy working from photographs, and the more there are, the better. I do enjoy their silence: no pleading requests to see the drawing; they are cooperative and courteous. I like to take an eye from this photo, a nose from that one and make a composite face that includes all the best (or rather worst) features available. The ideal situation would probably be to observe your victims through a one-way mirror, allowing them the freedom to be themselves and you, the artist, the luxury of uninterrupted solitude.

The business of drawing caricatures in public, whether for social or economic reasons, is a particularly difficult one. More than talent, patience and tolerance are required. You must gird your loins for a lot of artistic criticism from people who can't tell a watermelon from a grape. They will stand in back of you, squint critically and proceed to inform you that you have the eyes but you've missed on the mouth. You are tempted to say things like "Your mouth certainly isn't missing," but, no, you must bite your tongue and just hope they decide to sit in the hot seat so you can capture them on paper. That is your sweet revenge.

Others will impatiently ask, "Where are the ears?" I usually tell them quietly they're still in the pencil, and that seems to silence my inquisitors for a while. When doing caricatures in public, the most you can really hope to achieve is a quick impression that will satisfy the subject and your audience. A true caricature would take too long, and it requires more concentration than you're allowed in that situation. Think of the public caricature as a performance rather than an

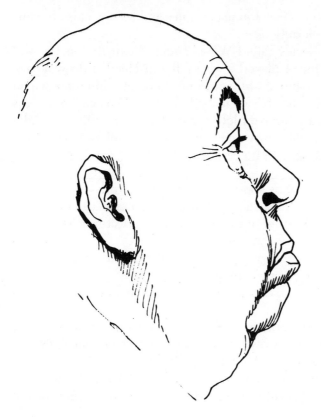

I took a stab at Hitchcock once, with this result.

Marshmallow skin. Flabby folds and a lower lip like a serving shelf. Eyes hiding a naughty secret. A gentle, self-contented sea lion.

When you are faced with a more even-featured, attractive face, you are forced to seize upon the tiniest imperfections.

In this case, I used her mouth and eyes and left the remainder of her face pretty much alone.

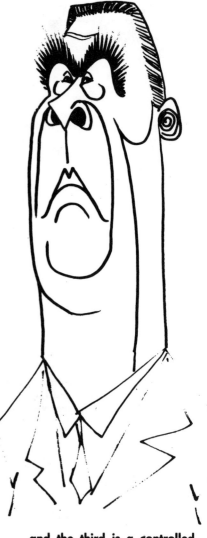

Here are three approaches to the face of Leonid Brezhnev. Each has its own unique appeal, and each technique has something different to say about the subject. As I've said before, the subject will dictate the technique to you. The first I did as a *portrait-charge* so that I could utilize subtle gradations to accentuate the craggy hills and valleys of his face.

The second is a rough sketch produced with a ball-point pen . . .

. . . and the third is a controlled design.

A timid face with a thin-lipped, eager smile.

Shining bird's eyes hiding behind a pair of horn rims.

Eyebrows become tentative smudges.

The pen-and-ink technique has a slightly harsher line, and it may add unwanted age to the subject of your drawing if you're not careful. I did these three children initially in pen, but I had to switch to pencil because their soft, unshaped features needed the nuances that pencil can bring.

These are my children Chrissie, Randy and Denise when they were but toddlers.

artistic accomplishment. Brevity and patience are most important, along with an engaging personality and some ability with a pen.

Children are instantly and innocently drawn toward cartoons and caricatures; they understand intrinsically the game being played with facial features—moving the nose up here, the eyes over there. This fits into their openly imaginative game plan more easily than it does into the thought patterns of the restricted, conventionally oriented adult. Caricature demands a childlike form of observation, and you have to get in touch with the child within you in order to feel the spirit of the art. Kris and Gombrich tell us in their essay on caricature that "reverting to the infantile in reducing a face to its comic essence is a form of child's play that acts as relief for the adult."

Children are not easy to caricature; their features are still rather amorphous. To me most babies look like either Winston Churchill or Oliver Hardy, cute and fat and funny-looking.

When drawing a child be sure to keep the head large—the body hasn't grown into it yet. The eyes are also large; the head and eyes remain fairly constant throughout the growth process, so they appear relatively larger in children.

One of the finest and clearest descriptions of what is required of a caricature is contained in the essay "Laughter" by Henri Bergson:

> The caricaturist who alters the size of a nose, but respects its ground plan, lengthening it, for instance, in the very direction in which it was being lengthened by nature, is really making the nose indulge in a grin. Henceforth, we shall always look upon the original as having determined to lengthen itself and start grinning.

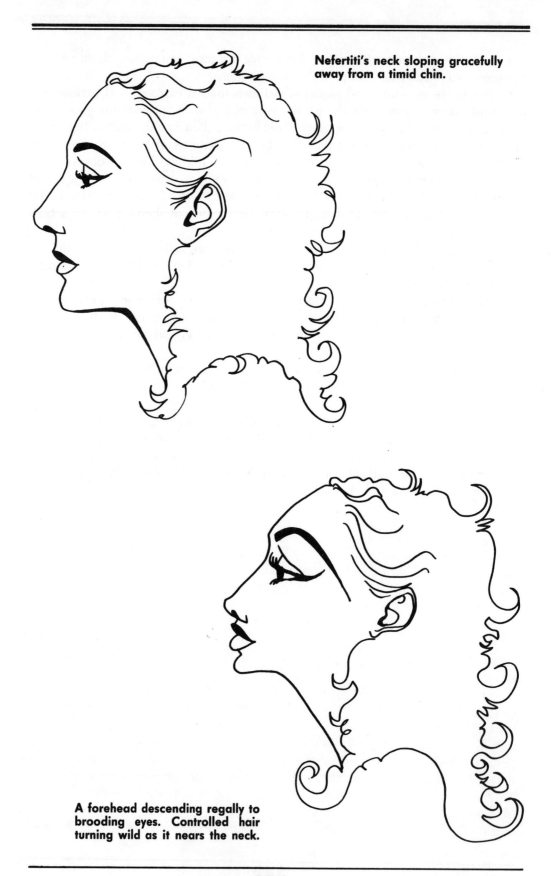

Nefertiti's neck sloping gracefully away from a timid chin.

A forehead descending regally to brooding eyes. Controlled hair turning wild as it nears the neck.

Afterthoughts

admit to being a compulsive rewriter. To make me relinquish this manuscript required the services of two sumo wrestlers and a team of paramedics. If it hadn't been wrested from my grasp, I would still be here making "just one more change." If this is beginning to sound like an apology, maybe it is. As I reflect upon this book I see all of the wonderful stories that I've failed to include and the talented artists that I've omitted (probably some of your favorites, darn the luck!). But look on the bright side: If I had included every worthy artist and anecdote, you'd need a U-Haul trailer to get the book home, and the price would be prohibitive.

The enjoyable, thoroughly satisfying thing about having written this book is recalling all of the books I had to read in order to write this one. I felt alternately smug and stupid from day to day as I discarded one tome and then discovered another. In the back of the book you'll find a list of the authors to whom I am deeply indebted. If I have been successful in whetting your appetite and you'd like to read more about the art of caricature, I can't recommend these books highly enough.

While I was writing and sketching and doing my research, one thought persistently gnawed at me: Art is essentially brave. Artists are a gutsy group. They defy convention, they dare to go their own way, to make their own statement. They are audacious and paradoxical: They thrive on acceptance but the very nature of their work invites criticism or rejection. Artists are strange birds. They produce and produce and then await the reviews. If the reviews are good, they return to work. If the reviews are bad, they shrug them off and still return to work. True grit is not confined to the Old West.

Yes, caricature is courageous and outrageous, and it's becoming more so every day. Our perceptions of art have changed, just like our tastes in music. What was disagreeably atonal yesterday is acceptable to our ears today. And so it is with art. I see our sociologically imposed "grid" slipping, and I mean that in the most positive way: We are gradually becoming more tolerant of those faces that don't measure up to our heretofore rigid standards of beauty. And America offers the widest variety of faces anywhere in the world. Everywhere we look we are treated to a stunningly diverse array of noses, brows, jaws, eyes, hair. America is a caricaturist's smorgasbord.

Yes, the old grid is slipping; this is clearly reflected in motion pictures, which are a sort of microcosm of our society. Today we accept stars with less than perfect faces; now we can worship people who look like people instead of gods. Barbra Streisand, Dustin Hoffman and Bette Midler are some of today's leading players who a few decades ago might have been relegated to playing comedy relief or maybe not playing at all. Our "slipping grid" is a giant step in the right direction. It indicates that we are less inclined to judge our fellow human beings by their covers, however "attractive" or "unattractive" they may be. We're giving them a chance to tell us who they really are inside.

Ever since Benjamin Franklin drew his "Join or Die," the United States has been a haven and a breeding ground for caricature. But then this is an unsafe art that can only thrive in a free climate. (The USSR is not noteworthy for its humorous arts.) I find it comforting to pick up the daily paper or a magazine and see a caricature of some powerful personage staring out at me. I always heave a quiet sigh of relief and think, "Well, freedom is with us for another day." Caricature is a fine yardstick for freedom. If ever the artist is censored, if our sense of humor or our opinion submits to the powers-that-be, if our stringent point of view is watered down, then we're really in trouble. I don't want to wave this flag too high, but imperfect though the country may be, the United States has survived and grown and retained her sense of humor and capacity for self-criticism. Let's hope it stays that way. As James Parton said in *Caricature and Other Comic Art*, "There must be something precious in caricature else the enemies of truth and freedom would not hate it as they do."

I hope this book has amused or enlightened you—preferably both—and I further hope that those of you with an interest in caricature will pursue it seriously, but not too seriously. We *need* good humorous artists in the world. In his essay "The Meaning of Comedy," Wylie Sypher wrote that "The comic spirit is the 'ultimate civilizer' in a dull insensitive world." He goes on to say that "it teaches us to be responsive, to be honest, to interrogate ourselves and to correct our pretentiousness."

From his mouth to God's ear.

Bibliography

Ashbee, C. R. *Caricature*. New York: Charles Scribner's Sons, 1928.

Auerbach-Levy, William. *Is That Me? A Book About Caricature*. New York: Watson-Guptill Publications, 1948.

Baudelaire, Charles. "L'Essence du Rire" (The Essence of Laughter). In *The Mirror of Art*, edited and translated by Jonathan Mayne. London: Phaidon Press, 1955.

Bergson, Henri. "Laughter." In *Comedy*, edited by Wylie Sypher. Garden City, N.Y.: Doubleday Anchor, 1956.

Blaisdell, Thomas. *The American Presidency in Political Cartoons: 1776–1976*. Exhibition catalogue. Berkeley: Berkeley University Art Museum, 1976.

Caruso, Dorothy. *Enrico Caruso: His Life and Death*. New York: Simon and Schuster, 1945.

Cross, Jack. *For Art's Sake*. Winchester, Mass.: Allen and Unwin, Inc., 1977.

Eastman, Max. *Enjoyment of Laughter*. New York: Simon and Schuster, 1936.

Feaver, William. *Masters of Caricature*. New York: Alfred A. Knopf, Inc., 1981.

Fry, Roger. *Transformations: Critical and Speculative Essays on Art*. 1930. Reprint. Garden City, N.Y.: Doubleday and Co., Inc., 1956.

Fuchs, Eduard. *The World in Caricature*. Berlin: A. Hofmann and Co., 1904.

Herford, Oliver. *Herford's Confessions of a Caricaturist*. New York: Charles Scribner's Sons, 1917.

Hess, Stephen, and Kaplan, Milton. *The Ungentlemanly Art: A History of American Political Cartoons*. 1968. Reprint. New York: Macmillan Publishing Company, 1975.

Kris, Ernst, with Gombrich, E. H. "The Principles of Caricature." In *Psychoanalytical Explorations in Art*. New York: International Universities Press, Inc., 1962.

Lancaster, Osbert. Introduction to *Max's Nineties: Drawings 1892–1899*. New York: J. B. Lippincott Co., 1958.

Lucie-Smith, Edward. *The Art of Caricature*. Ithaca, N.Y.: Cornell University Press, 1981.

McKim, Robert H. *Thinking Visually: A Strategy Manual for Problem-Solving*. Belmont, Cal.: Lifetime Learning Publications, Division of Wadsworth, Inc., 1980.

Meglin, Nick. *The Art of Humorous Illustration*. New York: Watson-Guptill Publications, 1981.

Meglin, Nick. *The Art of Humorous Illustration*. New York: Watson-Guptill Publications, 1981.

Mindess, Harvey. *Laughter and Liberation*. Los Angeles: Nash Publishing, 1971.

Murrell, William. *A History of American Graphic Humor*. New York: Whitney Museum of American Art, 1933.

Parton, James. *Caricature and Other Comic Art*. 1878. Reprint. New York: Harper and Row, 1969.

Rhode Island School of Design. *Caricature and Its Role in Graphic Satire: An Exhibition by the Department of Art at Brown University*. Exhibition catalogue. Providence, R.I.: Rhode Island School of Design, 1971.

Index

Note: Numbers in *italics* indicate illustrations.